# THE JOURNEY IS YOURS TO TAKE

# THE JOURNEY IS YOURS TO TAKE

## Choose to Move Through Frazzled to Fabulous

## An Anthology

CELESTE DUCHARME
ANNMARIE GRAY
PAM JOHNSON
SUSAN KERBY
SHANNON KING

# ADVANCE PRAISE

"What an amazing book! I literally could not put this book down. It is a far cry from your run-of-the-mill self-help books.

The authors shared, from very vulnerable places, their stories and how they moved from FRAZZLED to FABULOUS.

The stories were poignantly intertwined with challenge and encouragement.

The authors have been victorious through adversity and have developed a victor, not victim, mentality!

I believe anyone could benefit from reading this book; however, I encourage readers to dwell in places that speak to their heart; have a journal ready, and really dig in deep for ways to apply to their own life the wisdom that is shared. The willingness of the authors to share makes them highly relatable. The reader can feel that they are not alone in their struggles...that others have gone through similar things and came out on the other side—FABULOUS. These authors are willing to lay their hearts open so that the reader may benefit".

~ Daneen Ashworth, aPHR, SHRM-CP
HR Consultant
https://www.mycompasshr.com

---

"*The Journey is Yours to Take* reminded me that life's darkest hours can make us stronger and we, alone, have to make that choice! This book, with its five unique journeys and five powerful truths, shows us how to get back on track towards our dreams and on the road to greatness!"

Judy M. Bradbury
Certified Health and Wellness Coach,
Owner and Creative Director at JD Studios
judybradbury@gmail.com
https://www.instagram.com/judymbradbury
https://www.facebook.com/judy.m.bradbury

---

"We enjoyed the way this anthology was written and flows from topic to topic. It was easy to read and took little effort; we will save the effort to apply the wisdom found within! It is great to read about the varied life experiences of different women, compiled into one book, and wrapped around a common theme. It is obvious each author is passionate about mentoring and encouraging women to live their best lives. The work is authentic, and it was encouraging to see women address their hurts, habits, and hang-ups, and acknowledge their contribution to them. At the same time, as Shannon King's chapter so aptly points out, "our choice in how we respond to the AFTER is what defines us.

The advice offered is straightforward and practical. It also blends faith and psychology well—and by that we mean it is not overbearing on either extreme. It is obvious that faith and the Bible play a significant role in each author's life, yet the stories don't come across as denigrating or preachy as Christian or faith-based books sometimes do. However, it is also not fluffy; there is plenty of substance to this anthology that should make it a worthwhile read for many. We were pleased to find the writing was not overly technical and easy enough for laypeople to understand.

There is a Jewish proverb that states, 'Where there are no oxen the manger is clean, but abundant crops come by the strength of the ox.' There is little doubt that life is messy! But with faith, perspective, and a little help along the way, the messiness of life can be transformed into something beautiful. The authors of *The Journey is Yours to Take* move readers on a journey through their messes, trials, and mistakes, and share the nuggets of wisdom they've gleaned along the way. In the end, each is more FABULOUS for it, and their prayer is that you too will make the choice: FABULOUS over FRAZZLED as well. After all, each of us is *fearfully and wonderfully made*!

~Josh and Kim Kolstadt
Retired LE Sergeant
Foster/adoptive parents
Church Global Outreach Coordinator

"I so appreciate the true transparency, courage, and vulnerability shown through the stories of these five women. Thank you for sharing your journeys and the wonderful truths that have surfaced as you have chosen to overcome life's obstacles. This book inspires me to realize that I still have time to ask myself:

"Who am I?"
"Who do I want to become?"

As a stay-at-home mom, turned empty nester, this book could not have come at a better time for me! If you are looking for inspiration to restart, reshape, rethink, reenergize your life and relationships, this book is for you!

It's a powerful, raw, and honest view of those who honestly looked at their lives, who they were, who they would like to become—and made the necessary changes and adjustments to create lives that cherish joy, wholeness, fun, and delight.

Thank you, ladies, for having the strength of character to share your stories and helping me see that my story is not over, but that the best is yet to come!"

~ Eileen Nicholls,
Homemaker and Sales Specialist

---

I was touched by *The Journey is Yours to Take* because I could feel Celeste's authenticity and honesty in telling her story. She expresses her tough life experiences and uses them to help us (the readers) find hope in our own lives. Her list of favorite bible scriptures is a fantastic reference tool! Even the action plan is a huge benefit to readers. There are many inspiring quotes and acronyms to support the journey to live your dreams. This is a book you want on your shelf to refer back to over and over again. After reading this you will feel like you can accomplish anything!

Brooke Nunn
President | CEO
Temecula Valley Chamber of Commerce
brooke@temecula.org

---

"While you might not be able to join Pam Johnson on an actual outdoor adventure or therapeutic midweek hike, there's much to be gained by reading her upbeat expose on loss and addiction, growth and recovery, and the role of the outdoors in that process. Pam reminds us that loss is seldom within our control, but how we deal with it is.

Her unique contribution to this work is her concrete and specific suggestions for how to lean on others, seek referrals, make oneself the project and get outdoors for solace and rejuvenation; there are even a few recipes for campfire cooking!

More than just motivational talk, *The Journey is Yours to Take* is an empowering how-to for finding ways to incorporate friends and community members in outdoor activities and in practicing gratitude. As the world responds to post-pandemic healing, what better time for such guidance?"

Jennifer Helsel Shupper
Judge, California State Court

---

"So many of us can relate to Pam when she says, 'All the experiences in my life trained me to solve my own problems.' What a relief to be encouraged and given permission to use the four-letter word, HELP! Pam's challenge to MAKE YOURSELF THE PROJECT, by including others in your journey and by spending time in the best therapy sessions of all—the ones that happen while experiencing God's great outdoors, puts the reader on the trail to joy!"

Bonnie Sala,
President and CEO
Guidelines International Ministries

---

"I was moved by Johnson's authenticity, her ability to admit—to the world—the façade we try so hard to maintain: Our ability to be self-sufficient, independent, and in control of our lives, having it all, and being all-together. With amazing skills, Pam's chapter gently and compassionately shows the falsehood and cost of maintaining those beliefs, and how they rob us of opportunity, a sense of purpose, and the ability to grow and heal.

Johnson helps the reader feel safe and know they are not the only one who has felt alone and/or isolated. She goes further by providing practical tools and recommendations—ones that are easy to begin using, along with others that are also available at low or no-cost; eliminating a barrier we often confront when learning to take care of/investing in ourselves: money."

~ Kathy Drake,
Assistant Dean, Marketing and Communications
UC Riverside School of Business

---

"I completely relate to this piece from T*he Journey is Yours to Take*:

> "When I fell from grace, I fell hard. And I couldn't get up. I didn't even want to get up!"

I, too, have been there. For some reason, resiliency seems to fade as we get older, so the words and stories speak to me in such a relatable way. I so appreciate the raw description of isolation and shame. Yep, we've all been there. There is an elegant beauty to the glory that comes from ashes.

Readers might also relate to:

> "I am the one to take care of others in my family and work, multi-task, and work tirelessly."

I love Pam's healing through her outdoor adventures. The stories are uplifting with practical examples to inspire even the most frazzled among us."

Pia Hahn
VP, Corporate Communications

---

This anthology is an impactful read. If you can internalize and apply the information, it will be life-changing! Anyone who desires to better their lives, in terms of resilience and creating your own happiness, will want to read this over and over.

Shannon's section is easy to follow and impactful. The whole book is honestly amazing.

~Kelly Seda
Police Wife, Mom, and
Retired Police Officer.

---

"Such a testament to what strong women, coaches, mentors, and a COMMUNITY OF YOUR PEOPLE can produce—generations of strength, encouragement, support, and love! Celeste's struggles in life turned into a beautiful journey we can all relate to on many levels. I love her commitment to God and the many Bible verses of encouragement and redirection!

How many times have you felt FRAZZLED? It was refreshing to read how Celeste shared her vulnerabilities, yet showed us that in those times, we don't have to '…focus on being perfect; however, we must always embrace the will to never give in...to never give up. To CHOOSE JOY…,' but it's not always that simple, is it?

Thank you for giving us the tools, strategies, and encouragement in this book to believe in ourselves again, overcome life's often daily challenges, and focus on creating our best life…so we can all truly move from FRAZZLED to FABULOUS…no matter what life throws our way!"

~Kristine
Radio Personality, Voice Over Talent,
and often **FRAZZLED** Marketing Consultant…
focusing now on the FABULOUS!
KristineTurner.biz

---

Reading Susan Kerby's chapter I recognized myself in so many instances. While no one specifically told me I was *God's gift*, I felt the responsibility that it was my job to be a caretaker as the eldest daughter and sister, obliging cousin, industrious secretary, obedient wife, and doting mother. I wasn't special and my biggest goal in life was to be liked.

The message I received from this reading was clear—as a woman of faith, I am God's gift, and my life does revolve around me. By first knowing and loving myself, I am able to speak my truth. In being vulnerable in telling it, I get to use my words to share my message...with my voice, unapologetically and live my life with delight.

Mary E. Knippel
mary@yourwritingmentor.com
www.yourwritingmentor.com

---

"*The Journey is Yours to Take* is a life-changing experience.

The wisdom these five women share is magical. With it, I received a permission slip, practical tools, and guidance that every day gives me the choice to move through FRAZZLED to FABULOUS.

I finally found something I've been longing for my whole life: "DARE TO DREAM as if the world does revolve around you because yours does," as Susan Kerby shares. And I do dream thanks to The *Journey is Yours to Take.*

I invite you all to take this magical journey and COME PLAY."

Sofia Nunes, Founder
AwakenWhoYouAre.com

---

"Five women use their life experiences and wisdom to show you through their own hard knocks how to go from FRAZZLED to FABULOUS. The stories are so compelling, you'll almost forget you are reading a self-help book. The lessons are taught through the author's personal experiences. It feels like what we need is being transmitted to us within these pages.

~Sage Lee, Headmaster, The School For Wizards
theschooforwizards.com

---

"Loved the different perspectives of the authors...each giving me food for thought. Great examples to embrace and develop my own Frazzled to Fabulous!"

~Terry Carr
Partner, DecTec Properties, LLC

---

"At the onset of the Introduction, these words invite self-exploration, normalize experiences, and invoke a deeply motivating feeling to 'seek your personal best.'

The authors share their experiences traveling through FRAZZLED to FABULOUS. Each author shares steps and strategies useful in transforming one's life, peppering in affirmations and resilience, each designed to help one thrive and embrace a journey that weaves the intricate dance of FRAZZLED to FABULOUS. With an anthology like this, every reader will surely gain the wisdom to begin their own journey!"

~ Jenna Farrell
Educator, Wife, and Mom of two.

---

Each anthology drew us in. It was easy to relate to the writer's difficulties and triumphs. Their experiences helped us identify areas where we needed to have faith to persevere.

> Choices, always laid before us, where we have to trust our decisions. Resilience in times where quitting and taking the easy route seemed more appealing.

These incredible ladies tell their stories in a way that is relatable and through a lifetime of learning and dedication to improving themselves, they are now helping others live their best lives.

~ David Spencer
Retired California Highway Patrol Senior Motor Officer
~ Alicia Spencer
Realtor and career law enforcement wife to David

PRINT: 979-8-9853461-0-7

DIGITAL: 979-8-9853461-1-4

Annmarie Gray

Matters of Gray Press

555 Church St No. 2105

Nashville, Tennessee 31729

310-345-0065

Cover Designer: Patrick Sipperly

Printed in the United States of America

First Printing, 2022

10 9 8 7 6 5 4 3 2 1

*The Journey is Yours to Take* book is dedicated to each woman who may have an unspoken desire to belong...buried deep within her heart and soul.

—To each person yearning to be accepted, supported, encouraged, and taken in by a safe community of friends who will allow her to show up and be one hundred percent her true and unique self.

—To the brave and courageous individuals who face challenges, life's ups and downs, disappointments, and tragedies, yet believe—as the contributors of this anthology have discovered—no experience happens in vain. They were endured to bring HOPE for a FABULOUS future.

—To every reader who can hold in their hearts that our journeys were experienced and are now being shared, so that you will be inspired to boldly and confidently use the tools and strategies each author learned throughout her journey, with the sole purpose of now being able to share them with you.

Our hearts are filled with such gratitude to be able to dedicate this book to amazing, strong, and talented YOU, as you persevere and transition from feeling FRAZZLED to FABULOUS, time and time again.

*"Life is not easy for any of us. But what of that? We must have perseverance and, above all, confidence in ourselves. We must believe we are gifted for something, and that this thing must be attained."*

~ Marie Curie

# CONTENTS

# FOREWORD

*The Journey Is Yours to Take* is keenly relevant to our time.

While every life is fraught with difficulty, we now enter the third year of a global pandemic, continued economic uncertainty and disparity, social tension, and the polarization of seemingly every topic under the sun. We are swamped and steeped in *news* intended to trigger emotional response—anger, frustration, hatred, and fear. In general, we are overstimulated and under-resourced in the areas that matter. Where human connection is key to our survival, and while virtual connectivity is available to most, we have erected more and more barriers between us—both physical and psycho-social. When bombarded with so much that is truly out of our control, it's easy to feel overwhelmed and unable to improve our condition. With its emphasis on hopefulness, camaraderie, connection, faith, and tangible action, *The Journey Is Yours to Take* serves as an antidote to the forces that fracture our lives.

I too have chosen to counter those forces, having earned a degree in psychology from Duke University and other specific areas of associated study, served as a coach for over a dozen years, speaking on emotional resilience, and authored *Out of the Box—A Journey In and Out of Emotional Captivity*. Thus, I deeply appreciate the desire these women have to make a positive difference, offering themselves in service of others.

I had the honor of meeting the authors through my coaching work with Upside Thinking, where I saw firsthand their strength, resilience, and commitment to growth and helping others flourish. That commitment brought them together to share their insights and produce this remarkable book. Each woman recounts personal stories that are both candid and refreshingly devoid of self-indulgence, thereby creating a level of relatability and intimacy. The authors, each in her own right, are successful professional women who have had their own personal journeys and crafted unique solutions to despair, loss, and pain. The practices offered are never presented as a one-and-done magic pill. The intent remains modestly focused on where and how a person can choose to take action, even in small, pragmatic ways. Throughout the book the emphasis is on commitment and consistent action as integral to progress.

Aptly named, this collection offers perspectives on *life's journeys* and the wisdom to take that journey as gleaned personally and professionally from five uniquely talented women. Each writer delivers a chapter that interweaves her formative experiences and best strategies to navigate a wide range of life challenges—from deep emotional wounds to traumatic injury to the ravages of addiction and dependency. Before launching you into their loving effort to inspire us all to persevere on our journey into fabulousness, I will only add this: their circle of friendship and wisdom has enriched my life, and I'm confident it will enrich yours as well.

~Suzanne Dudley Schon
Life and Leadership Coach
https://www.suzannedudleyschon.com/

# ACKNOWLEDGMENTS

**IT CANNOT BE** understated how important the love, support, and attention to detail is to weave the dreams and stories of five women together in the hopes of touching the hearts of many. The list of all of those who stepped in and loved, supported, and offered their eyes for constructive review and their hearts for loving commentary is wide-reaching.

Without the support and love of our families, this book would not have been possible. We send huge gratitude to our spouses and children who encouraged our dream, put up with long absences while we wrote, and long calls while we collaborated. Words do not adequately express our love and devotion to you, nor can they fully convey how much you bless our lives.

We want to acknowledge the wonderful community of friends and professionals with which we find ourselves surrounded; we are sustained by your words of encouragement and motivated by your excitement. To those who responded to our request for the pre-reads and your advanced reviews with your elegant words of praise—you have touched our hearts.

To Suzanne Dudley Shon— from the very beginning of this journey, we were convicted you were the author for our Foreword. You succeeded in exceeding our expectations, which were already pretty elevated. We feel truly seen and humbled by your generous and eloquent expression that beautifully blends our stories and individualities to represent the community of powerful women in which we find ourselves so proud to be immersed.

Our deepest gratitude goes to Anna Weber, Literary Strategist and friend. Truly without you, this book would never have come to fruition. You educated, guided, and gently prodded in the necessary actions to write a book. You motivated and inspired us…and sometimes held our hands to keep moving forward. You held our dream for us. You are amazing and so greatly appreciated.

Our heartfelt gratitude goes out to each person who played a role in the creation of this dream, and to you, our readers, who have chosen to join us on this journey.

# INTRODUCTION

**WELCOME READERS! YOU** are in for a rich and fulfilling experience as you enjoy the stories of five very courageous women who share how they each have learned the choices that make it possible to shift through FRAZZLED to FABULOUS. It also sets the stage for you to build and nurture emotional growth through relationship, trust, and vulnerability—the kind of relationships rounded out by virtues these authors found within their journeys of doubt, pain, invisibility, and the two-sided coins of confidence, jubilation, and notoriety. You will quickly discover how the phrase, "If you only knew..." leads to an understanding of how this collective of authors has a great deal of empathy and each has lived through both highs and lows.

You will find a beautiful mix of good and bad experiences and perspectives of thriving within and through life challenges. Using the primary theme of shifting through FRAZZLED to FABULOUS, as viewed through the lens of "if you only knew," each author brings you poignant moments of meeting life's struggles through hurt, trauma, betrayal, etc., and embraces the vulnerability needed to share how they overcame life's trials.

In the stories, you will discover strong women who have overcome obstacles, which often left them FRAZZLED, ineffective and frustrated, yet transformed the beliefs and habits that left them living so it now feels FABULOUS! The undergirding of their stories lies in sharing journeys in quest of a *life you can hardly believe* and generously inspiring others to look for the miracles of purposefully living life for themselves.

This anthology would have little meaning if it had no core concepts, thus, you'll find a beautiful message woven, like a fine cloth, through humanity shared. You will see the threads of how we are all perfect and compelling in our strength and weakness, our power and our imperfection, our love, and our loathing…strong fibers, which show how persistence and partnership make the journey worth taking. A gift, indeed, as you learn how to persevere and thrive, even during difficult or FRAZZLED times.

This work is created with equal passion, compassion, and strategy; with the intention to share stories of struggles and triumphs so readers can take away examples that may work for them. This joining of a community as inspired writers led to greater understanding and confidence to explore together, with the ultimate goal to eliminate from the world the isolation that comes from struggling in silence.

If the writers have succeeded in their quest, *The Journey is Yours to Take* will deliver encouragement to thrive—through uplifting and positive messages that living a FABULOUS life is attainable through mindset, boundaries, and perseverance. It will clearly point out that FRAZZLED need not be a permanent state, and often there is a gift to be found within the FRAZZLED. If you only knew…becomes KNOWN as you discover where the authors came from and the gifts they share to apply to your life.

YOU will know the content of this anthology is meant for you if you find yourself transformed or get a glimmer of understanding about the difference positive change can bring to your life. You may:

come to know that change/transition can be invigorating and worthwhile.

discover the tools, strategies, and perspectives on how never to give in or give up.

experience hope, encouragement, and belief; or find the ability to create new opportunities as you find the courage to push through challenging times, and begin to dream, believe, and achieve.

There is immense value in learning that most people have serious challenges in life that come in many forms, even those who *look* like they have it all together (*If you only knew…*) and that it is very possible to elevate yourself from the seemingly lowest of lows to rise up and thrive—indeed, to live a fulfilling and fun life!

Ah! The sweetness of being perfectly transformed by challenges and triumphs and the myriad avenues for change that become visible—the joy of embracing change when you feel someone understands, can relate to your struggles, and provide hope for a different outcome. This transformation comes about by taking actionable steps to rise above your challenges and CHOOSING to be joy-filled…to take advantage of every opportunity to shift through FRAZZLED to FABULOUS.

You will know this anthology is written for you! It was not happenstance. Each story is penned by a woman who is passionate about taking you to a better place in life. You will read from one author how her life is one with many curves in the road; she feared the unknown and her desperate need to fit in led her to fortify her *less than* self-image. Her life was riddled with pain; thus, her story encourages you to feel the curiosity and invigoration within you—to imagine a world where everyone knows who they are, what they want, and how they impact others with their personal gifts. Sharing her lifelong trepidation of contribution, freedom, and whimsical existence, and the resulting experiences might invite you, as well, to recognize and embrace the possibility of shattering the mold in which you are uncomfortable—in exchange for living a life of purpose.

You may be the very reader who connects with a story written by the author who hopes that knowing the trials she went through can inspire someone else to be an overcomer who bravely turns new dreams into realities, regardless of their past. Or you may recognize the contributor whose drive and passion in life is to teach and share with others that we have a choice in how we respond to the challenges, struggles, and traumas that life delivers. Her intention is for you to come to believe through knowledge and understanding how you can build your resilience, elevate your mindset, and claim power in your life so you can be victorious over it!

The world is riddled with false beliefs…far too many of which we hold as truth. One chapter is the result of a contributor, compelled to share her story in this anthology because so many live under one of those false beliefs—that they cannot overcome experiences that have taken them down; they don't see how resilient we are designed to be. She is passionate to share a better belief—that you can choose to take discomforting, debilitating experiences and become even more resilient and prosperous in your life. You'll find the empowering message that "When in the middle of the FRAZZLED, my first step in calming myself is to stop WHINING "why me?" and start WONDERING "why me?" In many instances, my reply to God has been, "I hope this is useful to someone!"

---

*It is time to give a voice for others to hear.*

---

The words of wisdom, the life-changing gems in these pages are intended to lead you to seek YOUR personal best. Wisdom you will find in statements such as:

> "Turn yourself inside out, if only for a moment, to see what the world sees. Surprise yourself at the splendor the world sees you exude. Make your world a better place by embracing the magic of YOU! No permission required."
>
> "Live your best life, you deserve it!"
>
> "Celebrate adventuring! While my struggles have led me to get help, I have found these connections life-giving and continually surprising."
>
> "What takes me down does not HAVE to take me out…every day I rise up stronger!"
>
> "It always turns out well for me. Always. When I'm in the middle of the muck, I look to God and say, 'I can't wait to see how you get this one to turn out.'"
>
> "More to be revealed. There is always more truth to speak and more destiny to be revealed."

Yes, more is to be revealed. May YOU enjoy each chapter equally; may you find that for which you are searching, and may you learn how to take every opportunity to shift through FRAZZLED to FABULOUS.

# THE JOURNEY IS YOURS TO TAKE

# THE BLESSINGS OF A LEGACY

Celeste Ducharme

CELESTE ENCOURAGES, MOTIVATES, MENTORS, AND LEADS OTHERS BY EXAMPLE.

She has spent over three decades building businesses by managing teams within high-profile companies such as Dennis Uniform, Nordstrom, The Rancon Group, and Ranch RV & Self-Storage.

She and Roger, her husband of thirty-plus years, have raised two incredible children, Chad and Courtney. She is deeply grateful for the unwavering love and support of her entire family. Celeste is dedicated to her faith and loves helping others create amazing opportunities in their life.

CELESTE IS A SELF-STARTING, GOAL-ORIENTED, AND PASSIONATE LEADER.

As a top-ranked athlete, Celeste quickly learned not only how to be part of a team but how to push through obstacles. Her love of softball led her to coach athletes for over thirteen years. In this arena, she developed a passion for motivating others to pursue and achieve their dreams. Celeste is a co-author of the #1 International Best-Seller, *Turn Possibilities into Realities*, and will appear in the documentary *Beyond the Game*, produced by Susan Sember.

CELESTE HAS PROVEN HER EXTRAORDINARY SKILLS FOR SUCCESS.

Holding a degree in Business Administration, she uses both education and experience to provide valuable tools and strategies to promote success planning, which includes setting clear outlines for goals and developing daily action plans to achieve them. Building beauty from brokenness is a welcomed challenge for those who embrace her guidance.

A sought-after speaker, Celeste conducts annual Queen Making Experience Retreats and workshops for all women, regardless of their current life circumstances.

CELESTE BEGAN HER FAITH-FILLED JOURNEY IN 1991.

At twenty-three, Celeste made a life-changing decision to give her heart to Jesus. Learning how to trust in God for hope, love, favor, and provision has been transformative for Celeste. Through studying the *Word of God*, memorizing scriptures, surrounding herself with other Christ-centered praying women of faith, and listening to daily mediations faithfully, God has allowed her to persevere during the most difficult times and transition through being FRAZZLED to FABULOUS time and time again.

www.celesteducharme.com

# The Blessing of a Legacy

*I've learned that people will forget what you said, people will forget what you did, but people will never forget how you made them feel.*

~ Maya Angelou (1928 – 2014)
American poet, memoirist, and civil rights activist.

**IN LIFE, I HAVE** learned to believe in Charleston Parker's quote that you have three choices in life, "to give in, to give up, or to give it all you've got." It is a great reminder to be extremely grateful to have been left a legacy from my grandma and mom to never give in, to never give up, and to always give it all you've got. Unfortunately, it is a gift for which I did not always understand the value. I am blessed, however, as I pause and reflect on my life over the last three decades, that time and time again as I've transitioned from FRAZZLED to FABULOUS, the one constant in my success journey has been the belief in, and reliance upon, the empowering legacy given to me.

It is a legacy reflected in the empowering desire to be an overcomer regardless of trials, tribulations and roadblocks and it wasn't just given to me in a beautifully wrapped giftbox. Oh, no! I saw it being lived out around me in the ninety-four years of my grandma's life—and I still see it being lived out in amazing ways through the life of my eighty-year-old awesome and cherished mom! It is a legacy with a calling to be a strong woman of faith…not afraid of challenges or struggles. I was given the gift of being able to believe in myself and to achieve the success that is my birthright…my royal position, for such a time as this. Thank you, Lord!

Esther 4:14 tells us, *you have come to your Royal Position for such a time as this.* And for ME, today is that time.

You see, regardless of life's ups and downs, which may have come my way, I've retained a commitment to myself and to my heavenly Father: *to put in the work to be an overcomer and not be a person who gives up too easily or doesn't try*. The lives of my grandma and mom exemplify what courage is; always showing me that perseverance makes all things possible through both determination and consistent action. Another lesson that keeps nudging at me throughout life is that we need not focus on being perfect; however, we must always embrace the will to never give in…to never give up.

I've found it a challenge throughout my life to embrace and use the gifts and talent I have been given. I've found the balance to those challenges has been to surround myself with people whose support and belief in me have been the key to never giving up on living my dream life. What did I learn along the way? I acknowledge my journey may not always be easy; however, it will 100% be worth it.

You see, I have not always been able to see and embrace my gifts and talents. For many years I felt like quite a failure because I seemed not to hit the expectation or mark of perfection set upon me. That awareness makes me extremely grateful for my husband, children, coaches, teammates, colleagues, and friends in my life—each who has come alongside me over the years—each who picked me up, helped me analyze what went wrong when I fell or hit a wall, but never stopped believing in me.

Throughout my life's journey, one of the most important lessons I learned is just how much the quality of your community matters. Life puts before us many people who are not happy unless they are complaining or putting others down; thankfully, I learned over the years those are not my people.

As you read this book, my hope and prayers are that you will give yourself permission to listen to your heart and allow yourself to dream as though all things are possible. Yes, there will be times when you feel weighed down with frustration, bitterness, or anger. However, I fervently hope you will embrace the tools and strategies, which I share here with you…to assist you in creating your dream life and move through FRAZZLED TO FABULOUS, time and time again.

## STRATEGIES

*There will be obstacles. There will be doubters. There will be mistakes. But with hard work...there are no limits.*

~ Michael Phelps (1985 - )
American former competitive swimmer. He is the most successful and most decorated Olympian who holds the all-time record for Olympic gold medals.

**IT IS ESSENTIAL** that we are strategic in how we manage the transition in our lives. I trust you will be inspired by the ways hard work, doing life big, struggling with God's choices, finding courage, and dealing with anger, fear, and pain changed my own life!

## WHAT HARD WORK AND A NEVER-GIVE-UP ATTITUDE CAN DO FOR YOU.

**I AM BLESSED TODAY** to be living the life of my dreams. My husband Roger adores me, believes in me, supports me in DOING MY LIFE BIG, and loves watching me create amazing opportunities in my life. I am blessed that he sees me as HIS QUEEN. You know the delight I must feel to stop and realize that we have been married for over thirty years. We've embraced trials, tribulation, laughter, and memories together…and I am still greeted every morning with joy, a kiss, and my favorite morning tea.

To be honest, life has not always been this way; however, today I am so very humbled and grateful for his love and support in my life. I've come to receive these gifts because I choose every day to wake up with joy and express my thankfulness for the many amazing opportunities the Lord has given me.

In 2016, I began to see phenomenal business results of an eleven-year commitment as the Property Manager at a self-storage project, where I drew on the strength of my LEGACY to commit to a highly rigorous strategy of weekly connecting, marketing, teaching, coaching, rewarding my staff, and shifting with market demands—all through consistent action and determination. My commitment to customer services, integrity, and hard work allowed the Rancon Group to sell this self-storage business in excess of four million dollars over its appraised value. Did this sale mean my life was over? Was my dream at its end?

With deep gratitude I can share that following the sale of the self-storage company, instead of being let go and forced to find a new employment opportunity, the Rancon Group created a new position for me as Vice President of Self Storage Development, where I am now responsible for the property management at the

Rancon Group's newest one thousand-sixty-unit self-storage project Ranch RV & Self-Storage-French Valley. Opened in July of 2018, this beautiful facility reached full occupancy of ninety-five percent in just twenty-six months—ten months ahead of the industry standard for a facility this large—and during a national pandemic.

I guess you might say I've learned to like DOING MY LIFE BIG…the owners of the Rancon Group will proudly remember the spring of 2022 as the opening of another self-storage project. Ranch RV & Self-Storage of Temescal Valley will be the company's largest facility yet with thirteen-hundred units. Our strategy is to open two additional facilities: Ranch Self-Storage-Menifee, Idaho will open in 2023 and Ranch RV & Self-Storage-Winchester is slated for 2024.

Because…

> I choose every day to never give in, never give up, and to daily give all that I have…
>
> I confidently take the daily action steps necessary for my goals to connect and persevere…
>
> I surround myself with brilliant, self-driven, and amazing entrepreneurs…
>
> I refuse to let the naysayers' negativity stay in my head or stand in my way…

I have created my dream life and moved through FRAZZLED to FABULOUS time and time again. There are rewards for these choices I've found in uncommon hours…I also built a reputation for being a recognized transition specialist and property manager.

Six years ago, the lessons of my LEGACY and finding my stride by DOING MY LIFE BIG—sparked a fire inside! I listened to my heart's calling and founded a company where I could provide other women an opportunity to do something similar with their lives. Through A *Queen Making Experience Mentorship and Leadership* training program I have the privilege to teach women how to move through FRAZZLED to FABULOUS. It is one of my greatest joys to see these mentees create amazing opportunities in their life; it is with great pride I watch them step into creating their dream life.

What message does this leave for you, dear reader? There is a world of hope! With proper planning, a clear outline of your goals, and a daily plan of action, you can also move through FRAZZLED to FABULOUS and create a *Dream Life*. The evidence is there…it worked in my grandma's life, my mom's life, my life, my children's lives, and in the lives of women in business and athletes with whom I have worked.

Esther 4:14 tells us, *you have come to your Royal Position for such a time as this.* And for YOU, today can be that time!

## DOING LIFE BIG!

**TIME TRACKS QUICKLY** through our lives; sometimes we are in THE middle of a FRAZZLE, and then something occurs to quickly step us right into the FABULOUS! We need only be aware and willing when opportunity calls. The summer of 2019 was like that for me. I had the privilege of being interviewed about perseverance and my life's journey for a documentary film, *Beyond the Game*. This film is not only being picked up by Netflix but is also being shown to college student-athletes at universities and colleges across the nation. After four long hours of filming, one of the film's producers said "Celeste, when I first met you, I just assumed that your life was always just ROSES for you. Today, however, after having heard your story, I am amazed that through it all you always CHOOSE JOY; you consciously choose to keep picking yourself up and move forward…time, after time, after time."

In one of my favorite books, in Romans 8:28, we read that ALL things work together for good, for those who love the Lord and live according to HIS purpose.

I find hope in that message; I've learned to cling to it and by doing so I can now look back in my life—at all the challenges I was dealt—and with a grateful heart I now see just how faithful GOD has been to HIS promise, even through the most challenging times.

"What was there in my story that amazed the film producer," you ask?

I have to take you back in time to a devastating event, from which I bore the scars for many years. A simple time, really, when any girl celebrating her twelfth birthday would expect the day to be filled with the singing of *Happy Birthday* and the opening of coveted gifts. My joy was short-lived; the first present I so excitedly opened from a family member was a gift certificate to a weight loss center. I was old enough to realize I may have a few pounds to lose, but I was devastated. From that moment forward I took everything personally, and over time became more than just a little defensive with this person. I was further hurt when my mom made excuses for her saying, "She didn't mean it that way," or she would try to assuage my defensiveness, saying, "She just wants you to look your best." Neither my mom nor I realized how that *gift* and the ongoing comments like these would eat away until all resemblance of self-esteem was eroded.

I was a pain-filled teenager who chose to drink, trying to drown out the pain and hurt, which had hurdled its way into my life. Maybe you'd like to know what a typical day in my fourteenth year looked like for me.

I would get up, head into the kitchen, take a glass of orange juice from the kitchen, walk over to my parent's mini-bar, and put half a pump of vodka in it. The problem didn't resolve itself with time; added age most certainly wasn't accompanied by either maturity or wisdom! Once I drove in high school, barely sixteen years old, I could be found with some frequency walking into the local liquor store close to my home in Orange, California, where I found it too easy to purchase my fill of beer and wine coolers. Yes, with some frequency...almost every Friday and Saturday night, yet I was never once carded. You see drinking and looking for affection from boys, who would say, "I love you" even if they had only one intention, was my way of attempting to take control of my life.

---

*I can look back now and see I had Guardian Angels surrounding me;*
*I probably have no business being alive today.*

---

Another fast forward, and you can find me at twenty-eight, excited to attend my ten-year high school reunion. Probably like most graduates, my excitement was framed around the PREPARATION for the night. I mean, I was going back to see all those old classmates, so I put on a new dress, got all dolled up—from the top of my head to the bottom of my toes. Of course, I walked in feeling amazing and still felt pretty great when I was approached by three girls who had been the popular cheerleaders. They said, "Hi" and "Wow, Celeste, it is really great to see you."

Still feeling good, I responded, "Oh, it's great to see you too."

But I guess the world has a way of bringing one back to reality. At least mine did, because the remaining girl stepped closer, gave a bit of a quiet stare, and offered her greeting, "Celeste? I thought you would be dead by now."

From this ugly and painful realization, it was clear and evident…I did have guardian angels around me. Nor will I EVER forget her words or the feeling of gratefulness that came over me after my head cleared from being stunned by her words. I was protected by my Heavenly Father during all the years of making bad choices and my life was spared—by His best choice. It is human to be surrounded by our blessings and not fully recognize them; sometimes it takes a wake-up call to turn our thoughts in a different direction.

Over the next year, I began to open my heart and mind to the realization that God had a purpose for my life. The greater awareness was how all those challenging years, all the times I did so poorly at enduring extreme pain and suffering, would someday be used for HIS glory.

## STRUGGLING WITH GOD'S CHOICES

IN 1995, I lost my father to liver disease. I was twenty-seven years old, hurt, and extremely angry at God. Like any loving daughter, I had prayed continually for God to heal my dad, but He didn't. I struggled *big-time* with God's choice to take my dad from me. Over the course of about two years, and after many angry conversations with God, He spoke in a very calm voice saying, "Celeste, I did not answer your prayers because I answered your dad's wishes. I can still hear how lovingly he spoke to me, as he further explained, "Celeste, your dad was in pain, he had lost everything, and he was ready to go HOME."

As you can well imagine, I felt like a spoiled brat…not thinking about what my dad was going through because being held in the depths of my hurt and pain all I could think of was myself. However, reflecting often over the years about my relationship with my dad, I have been able to recognize the unconditional love

I received from him throughout my life was priceless. I've also come to know with the greatest confidence the love and trust I had with my dad is ultimately what led me to have an incredible relationship with my Heavenly Father.

## THE COURAGE TO BOUNCE BACK

WHEN THE ECONOMY turned in 2008, my husband's job was then dissolved in 2009 so he *took the summer off* to enjoy some quality time with our kids. However, as summer drew to a close, he found the economy had become unstable and jobs were difficult to find. There was no way to foresee how these changes would affect our family, or my husband…mentally. We had little choice but to face the challenges of this downturn and all that followed, such as losing our home in 2010.

At this point, Roger and I had to make some very tough life decisions: where we would move to, how we would even get into another home, faced with our broken finances, and most importantly, how we'd bounce back within our marriage.

I can look back now at that horrendous and terrible time and see the amazingly strong marriage that God gave us through it all! I have also come to realize that the pain, the lessons learned, and every day embracing the NEVER GIVE IN AND NEVER GIVE UP mindset was absolutely worth it!

## ANGER, FEAR, AND PAIN—OR FAITH

IT WAS TO be expected when twenty-five years of being both a three-sport athlete and coach had finally taken its toll on my body, that pain would be a part of my life.

My choice to give up what I had loved doing for twenty-five years could have broken me; however, I knew deep inside that living in pain was not the LEGACY I'd been given, so embracing faith was my only option. I had to boldly address my choices: fear versus faith, and I recalled how often I'd seen the acronyms for each.

| | |
|---|---|
| **F**alse | **F**ull |
| **E**vidence | **A**ssurance |
| **A**ppearing | **I**n |
| **R**eal | **T**he |
| | **H**eart |

That was on my mind when in August, 2012 I went in for a routine knee replacement, which unexpectedly came loose in 2013. In 2014, I went in for a second knee surgery for a partial replacement, which came loose in 2015.

I became so very angry and frustrated, to say the least, because the knee replacement was supposed to take away the pain, not create more. I had become100% frustrated, which led me to ask myself over and over again, "What is wrong with me?" and "How could this be happening to me?" And then…in July of 2016, I had a third knee replacement, which failed me again as it came loose in 2017.

The anger, disappointment, pain, and fear of what was next and how I would resolve the problem held me in the grips of devastating emotions and frequently had me awash in tears. Fortunately, I knew my only option was to never give in, never give up and give it all I've got!

I sought help from my primary care physician for additional medical opinions, so I could have all three of my prior surgeries reviewed by a specialist outside of my medical group. I was put in touch with a doctor who reviewed my full medical surgery history and provided me with information to share with my orthopedic surgeon. This material mirrored the feedback and opinion held by my current doctor's Medical Board of Directors, who carefully reviewed and collectively agreed on what would be the best procedure to make this next knee replacement, my last.

Thus, on March 26, 2018, I found myself under surgery once again for what I prayed would be my final full knee replacement. As I came out of recovery, based on prior experiences, I knew there was something definitely wrong. I had no feeling or movement in my left foot. Yet the doctor's first comment when he came in to check on me was, "Oh, there is nothing to worry about. Just give it a few days and you will have that feeling back!"

Each day found me more disheartened as my one-day hospital stay turned into two. Three days turned into four. I wasn't sure what my attending physician would think about me being up and walking around with a walker on day four, still having no feeling or movement in my left foot or toes. By day five I no longer cared what he would think! All I wanted to do was go home, hide, and cry until my emotions were spent.

Time heals the worst of pain-filled moments and today as I look back on the outcome of my surgery and what I had before me, I am grateful I can remember the best parts of an otherwise terrible experience. I value the love and support of my mom, husband, children, and friends. Without them, my story would have a different ending; I would never have made it through the time necessary to heal. I will forever remember every loving person who came to our home to bring us food, stop in for visits, pray for me daily, and cheer me on. In those dark moments, it was my greatest blessing to have them support me emotionally and prayerfully, when I felt like little more than a broken mess.

In retrospect, I can now acknowledge I was filled with tremendous self-doubt and anger, and yet as one by one my friends, mom, children, and husband spoke words of hope, healing, and faith into me, my negative feelings dissipated. The shift toward hope, healing, and faith they provided is what got me through the nightmare of a fourth knee replacement and the neuropathy, which tried daily to steal my joy, drive, and purpose in life.

Also in retrospect, I accept how the medical situation slowed me down. The need to learn to walk when I had no feeling in my left foot and toes demanded I give more. More to a daily commitment to meditation, reading scriptures, and the movement and muscle memory exercises, which, over the last three years allowed me to regain sixty-percent use of my toes and foot. My doctor had changed his diagnosis from, "Oh, there is nothing to worry about. Just give it a few days and you will have that feeling back"—to telling me—"Walking with feeling in your foot might not be possible." The *slowing down* and the *miracles* that came through it urge me to give thanks daily and all the glory to my awesome and faithful God!

The *slowing down* has also helped me better see God work miracles in my life time and time again and I know that He wants to do the same in your life. It also helped me to see now that God has been preparing me throughout life—to answer His calling for me: To teach tools and strategies to women so they, too, can also move through FRAZZLED to FABULOUS and be an overcomer. I realize it will not be easy; however, I believe it will be worth it.

Struggle, challenges, and times of transition...they are a natural part of one's life and provide us the greatest lessons. One of mine is to have learned to count them all as joy, as admonished us in James 1:2: *Count it all joy when you fall into various trials.* I have also learned that our plans are NOT always HIS, and I have learned to praise GOD for this and embrace the belief, "Your will be done, Lord."

As I look back over the last four decades of my life, I have never stopped having to transition or deal with change, challenges, struggles, or pain. However, I have learned to look at these essential changes as my life is being REDIRECTED—and that it is not the end of the world when my life sometimes turns to FRAZZLED. Moreover, I LOVE that today I get to contribute daily to women who struggle with circumstances that take them out of the joy-filled life, which God has waiting for them.

Today, my life is rich and full, knowing the outcome of my life's journey was never intended to be about perfection. Rather, it was designed to teach me how…time and time again, I moved through FRAZZLED to FABULOUS because of our awesome loving and powerful God. It was God's plan to remind me of the amazing LEGACY given to me as a young child: to never give in, never give up, and give it all I've got! I now fully understand I would not have arrived at this point of my life without my faith, family, friends, and determination to persevere, live the life of my dreams with passion and purpose, and to honor God in all circumstances.

## FEARLESS SOUL

*Promise me you'll always remember: You're braver than you believe and stronger than you seem, and smarter than you think.*

A. Milne (1882 – 1956)

An English writer noted primarily as a playwright before the huge success of Pooh overshadowed all his previous work.

TO BEST UNDERSTAND where you are going in life, you must have a fearless soul that knows its purpose. Many people shy away from connecting with their purpose in life; they feel it may be complicated, complex, confusing. *Au Contraire*! It is simple: your life purpose consists of what motivates you—the reasons you get up in the morning. It creates a fearless soul, guides our life decisions, influences behavior, shapes our goals, provides direction, and verifies deeper meaning in life.

As I wrestled with my life purpose, I found it all neatly wrapped up in three components: my how, my why, and my faith.

## MY HOW

AT A VERY young age, I was taught by my uncle, that "Goals don't GET you anywhere in life, Celeste. They TAKE you everywhere." I was also taught to set goals and how to create action steps each day, which would lead me to ACHIEVE my goals. You see, my capacity to set goals and create a plan of action to achieve them has been one of the biggest keys to my success. It has allowed me to transition time and time again in my life, with ease and grace.

## MY WHY

MY HUSBAND AND I have two wonderful children who we raised to DREAM, BELIEVE, and work hard to ACHIEVE. Our son, Chad, is twenty-nine years old and is the Société Operations Manager at Europa Village & Winery in Temecula, California. Chad worked hard to mix academics and sports; he earned his business degree while on a football scholarship at Bacone College located in Oklahoma. It has been the five well-deserved promotions he received since completing his college degree, which led him to his current position.

Needless to say, my husband and I are exceptionally proud of our son. Chad calls me regularly and on one of our more recent calls he said, "Hey, Mom, I called so I could share something with you." My heart swelled as I heard the pride in his voice when he continued, saying, "Mom, I just celebrated my eighth year at Europa and as I sit here at my desk looking over my goal sheet, I realize I've achieved every promotion that I set out to reach. Mom, it happened!"

Time stopped for just a moment, and as tears filled my eyes, I finally cleared the choking in my voice and said to him, "Chad, you know you truly deserve these achievements. It was you, and you alone, who made each one happen, and each was through your hard work, a deep commitment to clear communication, and always taking constant daily actions…YOU made this happen, Son!"

In May 2021, joy and love filled our hearts as our daughter, Courtney, received her Degree in Elementary Education from Cornerstone University in beautiful Grand Rapids, Michigan, where she had previously accepted a softball scholarship. Courtney was placed in the position to complete her junior year online, and her softball team could not compete on the field for their spring 2020 season due to COVID-19. My pride in her knew no bounds when she took control over what she could, packed up her college apartment and regardless of the stress of the pandemic—embraced her college classes online with strength and courage. You can imagine my joy when I saw my family LEGACY sparked in my daughter and saw in her a *living encouragement* to others as she continued to embrace her leadership roles on the softball team as a captain and also served on the college Student-Athletes Leadership Team.

Courtney has worked hard on the field and in the classroom her entire life to achieve her dreams of being a college scholarship athlete and teacher. Perseverance and trust in God's faithfulness have remained the foundation of her journey. Yes! That same *never give in and never give up* legacy was most assuredly handed down to her.

Joy in your children comes in many ways over the years. The next sequence of events was Courtney's engagement to Tate in October of 2019 and their fairytale wedding day on October 1, 2021. Beyond the joy is the peace I feel that she has been welcomed into an amazing and caring family of faith, who have made accepting Grand Rapids, Michigan her home much easier. There was a beautiful strength and confidence visible in Courtney as she completed the last semester of her senior year of college, planned her dream wedding, stepped into her dream career of being a teacher, and now embracing one of Gods greatest gifts of all…Tate and Courtney will become parents in October of 2022.

Courtney's journey required perseverance through myriad injuries, and the stress of changing high schools that is never easy. However, as her mom, watching her DREAM, BELIEVE, and work hard to ACHIEVE the desires of her heart, has been one of my life's biggest blessings.

I know many times during my life when things have been in a somewhat FRAZZLED state, others would ask me, "Why do you continue to push through when things, Celest, when they become so challenging?"

The answer is easy. Each day, I look at my goals and ask myself the same question, "Celeste, why is accomplishing this important and how will this better life for our family and our future family LEGACY?" My *why* is embedded deep in my heart; I have learned to embrace life's challenges with perseverance, and with joy, passion, and purpose—because of my treasured children and generations to come."

## My Faith

**Most often in** life, we rarely know another person's struggles because we've been taught to keep them to ourselves—to look good and to make life look easy. However, God knows it all and I have learned to trust Him. Every day since Jan 6, 1991, when I gave my Heavenly Father my life and invited Him into my heart, I've worked to establish a relationship with Him and to rely on His word. My God is my strength, my courage, and my grace. He is all things love and the provider of peace. It is upon these truths I have learned to rely on and trust in Him...because of what His word represents.

To be able to move through Frazzled to Fabulous time and time again and have the ability to persevere, the first thing I had to learn to overcome was fear. I realized the only way to conquer fear was to faithfully put my trust in God every day. It is interesting how a simple choice became easier with each step of one's journey, and even more fascinating to see so clearly how faithful God is. I cherish the knowledge that God's word does not go void—it is my rock upon which to stand—and His words are promises to each one of us.

Living in fear and worry is time spent on a debt you and I may never have. It's true! I encourage you to give some thought to certain things upon which you've spent hours, days, or weeks worrying about, which never came to be. To further encourage you in this consideration, I want to share gems, which I read on a monthly basis to keep my mind and heart focused on our awesome and faithful God.

> *Isaiah 41:10: Fear not, for I am with you; be not dismayed, for I am your God; I will strengthen you, I will help you, I will uphold you with my righteous right hand.*

*Psalms 91:4: He will cover you with his feathers and under his wings you will find refuge; his faithfulness will be your shield and rampart.*

*2 Tim 1:7 For God hath not given us the spirit of fear; but of power, and of love, and of a sound mind.*

*1Thessalonians 5:16-18 Rejoice always, pray continually, give thanks in all circumstances; for this is God's will for you in Christ Jesus.*

*2 Thessalonians 3:16 Now may the Lord of peace himself give you peace* **at all times** *and in every way. The Lord be with all of you.*

*Psalm 100:5-5 For the Lord is good and his love endures forever; his faithfulness continues through all generations.*

*Philippians 4:6-7 Do not be anxious about anything, but in everything by prayer and supplication with thanksgiving let your request be made known to God. And the peace of God which surpasses all understanding, will guard your heart and your minds in Christ Jesus.*

*2 Thessalonians 3:3 But the Lord is faithful, and he will strengthen you and protect you from the evil one.*

*James 1:12* **Blessed is the one who perseveres** *under trial because, having stood the test, that person will receive the crown of life that the Lord has promised to those who love him.*

*Prov 31:25 She is clothed with strength and dignity, and she laughs without fear of the future.*

---

There may be times when you will find the need for more strength when called upon to embrace and use the talents God has given you. When I find myself in this situation, I rely on these passages:

*1 Peter 4:10 10 Each of you should use whatever gift you have received to serve others, as faithful stewards of God's grace in its various forms.*

*Colossians 3:23* And whatever you do, do it heartily, as to the Lord, and not to men.

*Ephesians 2:10* For we are God's masterpiece. He has created us anew in Christ Jesus, so we can do the good things he planned for us long ago.

*Romans 8:37* Know, in all these things we are more than conquerors through him who loved us.

*Philippians 4:19-20* And my God shall supply all your needs according to His riches in glory by Christ Jesus. Now to our God and Father be glory forever and ever. Amen.

*Psalm 16:8* I keep my eyes always on the Lord. Within at my right hand, I will not be shaken.

*Proverbs 31:29-31* Many women do noble things, but you surpass them all. Charm is deceptive and beauty is fleeting but a woman who fears the Lord is to be praised. Honor her for all that her hands have done and let her works bring her praise at the city gates.

---

**LIFE IS NOT** lived in a vacuum; we need others, whether or not we like to give up our independence. When I need to be reminded of how important it is to surround myself with people who believe in me, I read these words of wisdom:

*1 Corinthians 15:33* Do not be deceived: Bad company ruins good morals.

*Proverbs 13:20* Whoever walks with the wise becomes wise, but the companion of fools will suffer harm.

*Jeremiah 3:15* And I will give you shepherds after my own heart, who will feed you with knowledge and understanding.

*Proverbs 27:17* Iron sharpens iron, and one man sharpens another.

---

**Walt Disney is** well known for living his belief that "All our dreams can come true if we have the courage to pursue them." If I should find myself needing to focus or clarify goals and embrace my dreams, I remind myself of the messages that have long held me strong.

> <u>Hebrews 13:5-6</u> *Regardless of your season, you can count on God's faithfulness. He says, I will never leave you nor forsake you. So, we may boldly say: The Lord is my helper; I will not fear.*
>
> <u>Hebrews 13:21</u> *May He equip you with all you need for doing his will. May he produce in you, through the power of Jesus Christ, every good thing that is pleasing to Him. All glory to Him forever and ever! Amen.*
>
> <u>Psalm 18:2</u> *The Lord is my rock, my fortress, and my deliverer; my God is my rock in whom I take refuge, my shield and the horn of my salvation, my stronghold.*
>
> <u>Proverbs 18:10</u> *The name of the Lord is a strong tower; the righteous run to it and are safe.*
>
> <u>Psalm 20:4</u> *May he grant you your heart's desire and fulfill all your plans!*
>
> <u>Matthew 7:7-8</u> *Ask, Seek, Knock...*
>
> *(7) Ask and it will be given to you; seek and you will find; knock and the door will be opened to you.*
>
> *(8) For everyone who asks receives; the one who seeks finds; and to the one who knocks, the door will be opened.*
>
> <u>Psalm 33:20</u> We put our hope in the Lord. He is our help and our shield.
>
> <u>1 Corinthians 16:13</u> Be on your guard; stand firm in the faith; be men of courage; be strong.

Deuteronomy 31:6 Be strong and of good courage, do not fear nor be afraid of them; for the Lord your God, He is the One who goes with you. He will not leave you nor forsake you.

Psalm 27:1 The Lord is my light and my salvation; whom shall I fear? The Lord is the strength of my life; of whom shall I be afraid?

Jeremiah 29:11 For I know the plans I have for you declares the Lord, plans to prosper you not harm you; plans for hope and a future.

## ACT TO ACHIEVE

*It is easy to sit up and take notice, what is difficult is getting up and taking action.*

~ Honore de Balzac (1799-1850)

French Novelist

**ARE YOU READY** to stop making excuses, be an action-taker, and move through FRAZZLED to FABULOUS?

One of the most important steps you need to take to shift your life's path through FRAZZLED to FABULOUS is to be willing to embrace your dreams and the life-changing impact they will have upon you. It is time to move through FRAZZLED to FABULOUS and create an action plan to turn your dreams into reality.

Are you ready to do this? If so, then this chapter shows you the tools and strategies to accomplish that! What an opportunity this chapter is! You can take time for yourself, time for your dreams, time to decide if you could create your dream life, what it would look like…within your relationships, your career, and how you take care of yourself.

This may be the first time you've ever given yourself permission to DREAM BIG…the first time to put your faith to the test, living your life as THOUGH ALL THINGS ARE POSSIBLE, and being mindful of the empowering phrase in Philippians 4:13 *I Can Do All Things Through Christ Who Strengthens Me.* This may also be the biggest challenge you've ever undertaken…to dream with the underlying belief that God has great plans for you, as he confirms in Jeremiah 29:11 *For I know the plans I have for you, declares the Lord; plans to prosper you and not to harm you; plans to give you hope and a future.*

This section of my chapter is action-packed! It is designed to shift you away from merely THINKING about things, going beyond DECIDING, to TAKING forward-moving steps.

*A goal without a plan is just a wish.*
~ Antoine de Saint-Exupéry (1900 – 1944)
French writer, poet, aristocrat, journalist, and pioneering aviator.

**THINK ABOUT THIS** concept: we all tend to make a lot of decisions, such as eating healthier, getting a degree, changing careers, or starting a new business. However, *decisions* mean little to nothing…until we move from DECIDING to DOING! It is necessary to develop a habit of TAKING ACTION; it is with a finely tuned habit of putting ideas and decisions into ACTION we can accomplish big dreams.

*"Your beliefs become your thoughts; your thoughts become your words;*
*your words become your actions;*
*your actions become your habits;*
*your habits become your values;*
*your values become your destiny."*

~Unknown

**AS WE MOVE** through this section, ask yourself important questions to determine if you are ready to STOP!

Stop waiting until conditions are perfect?

Stop, get up, and do it?

Stop over-thinking things—and believe in your dreams?

Stop wavering and take continuous action?

Stop giving in to fear and use your action to overcome it?

Stop looking at your past and focus on the present?

Stop allowing distractions to prevent you from being actively engaged in doing.

*A dream written down with a date becomes a goal, a goal broken down into steps becomes a plan, a plan backed by action becomes reality.*

~ Dr. Greg Reid

Award-winning author, keynote speaker, and film producer.

## ARE YOU READY?

**YOUR FIRST ACTION** step is to grab a journal or several pieces of paper and spend ten minutes writing down your dreams in the areas of your relationships, career, and how you take care of yourself.

After you have written down your dreams, I can only imagine that some elements of fear may have snuck up on you. So here is where the next step is put into play and reveals how you can let go of fear and learn to persevere.

It might be FEAR of what people think...

FEAR of what people may say...

FEAR of how someone will react to you embracing moving through FRAZZLED to FABULOUS...

Or maybe the simple FEAR of failing...

It is time to embrace the important step that will help you LET GO OF FEAR. Let's look again at fear, which is truly:

**F**alse<br>
**E**vidence<br>
**A**ppearing<br>
**R**eal

The word fear or failure may be holding you down like a ton of bricks, and I want to encourage you to let go of fear today. Have you ever heard the analogy that *letting go of fear is like taking one brick at a time out of a very heavy backpack you've carried around for way too long?*

Have you ever considered that part of letting go of fear is to understand what might happen if you do LET GO of the pain, the bad memory, or a prior bad experience? What if...by letting go, opportunities become endless, and you can move through FRAZZLED to FABULOUS with ease? Wow! How awesome would that be?

Far better than the alternative! Just imagine what your life might look like if you don't decide to let go of fear. Can you imagine the weight on your shoulders? Can you imagine a life with little joy? Can you imagine how difficult it is merely to function from day to day?

The next action I want you to take is to look differently at the word FAIL and commit to no longer allowing it to hold any power over you; no longer allow it to frustrate you. Look at it instead as the first attempt in learning.

**F**irst

**A**ttempt

**I**n

**L**earning

Any time you feel you've failed, look at it as a time to assess the event as an opportunity to learn. Then, when you embrace the possibilities, you are much more inclined to take action and stick to your plans and goals, no matter what the outcome. When you believe you learn from experiences the rewards are great…amazing things will come from that belief. It is also a good time to look at life through the words of Romans 8:28, which says, *all things work together for good.*

How you begin to let go of fear is by trusting the process and the journey God has for you. GOD'S GOT YOU and He wants you to TRUST HIM. As you may have understood from other parts of my story, one of the most powerful and life-changing things I have done in my life is to have faith in our awesome, loving, and faithful God. COURAGE has never been about the absence of FEAR; it is, instead, the presence of FAITH. Stop a moment and consider this carefully, and then, ASK yourself, "Is it time to TRUST God that He will help me create a roadmap to move through FRAZZLED to FABULOUS and turn my dreams into realities?"

---

Are you *READY* to *LET GO* of the *FEAR* that has kept you playing *SMALL*?

---

That is an important question, and if your response is, "yes," then it's equally important to be one hundred percent honest with yourself and figure out what stands in the way of you letting go of FEAR, what prevents you from turning your dreams into reality, AND what stalls you in the exciting move through FRAZZLED to FABULOUS?

Is it your **ATTITUDE**? The action necessary to modify your attitude is to rid yourself of negative self-talk. STOP yourself whenever you think or say, "I CAN'T do this," or, "I will NEVER be good enough."

Is it your **EMOTIONS?** When you feel the emotions envelop YOU, remember that you have the CHOICE to STOP. STOP the pity parties; STOP being so sensitive to feedback and learn to embrace the feedback that builds champions!

Is it your lack of **FAITH?** It is within your ability, through a willingness to learn from your past, to not let a LACK OF FAITH own you!

Throughout life, you will with some frequency make personal assessments as you seek to determine what is STANDING in your way. Once the *culprit* is discovered, you then have to commit to persevering with your thoughts, your WORDS, and your actions.

## WHO DO YOU WANT TO BE?

**REMEMBER, IT IS** always YOU who has both the privilege and responsibility to choose when and how you DO LIFE! I can give you all the tools in the world; however, without your WILLINGNESS to be an ACTION TAKER and without a deep **F**AITH in God and the process, LITTLE WILL HAPPEN.

---

*It is YOUR time to shine, move through*
*FRAZZLED to FABULOUS*
*and embrace FAITH.*

---

## FULL ASSURANCE IN THE HEART

**DID YOU NOTICE** the acronym for FAITH?

FULL

ASSURANCE

IN

THE

HEART

Let's do a little more than just *take notice*; this is another of those action steps, which will turn your life in yet another beautiful direction. Are you ready?

It's time to take action…get a blank piece of paper on which to write down a few things. First, embrace the reality: if you want to create DIFFERENT RESULTS in your life, it is vital to teaching yourself NEW PATTERNS, which will create clear and positive changes in your life. It's time now to take a few minutes and write the things you want to LET GO of in your life. Maybe it is any one, or many of the following:

Stress.

Unforgiveness.

Anger.

Bitterness.

A crazy life that calls for you to slow down!

Write down whatever keeps you from moving through FRAZZLED to FABULOUS or prevents you from creating amazing opportunities in your life. Once you have described your thoughts on paper…stand up and crinkle the piece of paper up into a ball and throw the paper with the stinking thinking on it across the room and allow yourself to *feel* the release! Get rid of it! Put the stinking thinking in the garbage where it belongs.

---

*Didn't that feel great!*

---

I ask you again, "Are you ready to LET GO of FEAR and move through FRAZZLED to FABULOUS? Are you ready to start living your life with absolute JOY, not FEAR, and boldly embrace Proverbs 31:25, which enlightens us: *She is clothed with strength and dignity, and she laughs without fear of the future.*

As I encourage you to *be ready,* I want to address a few things which matter in the actions YOU take on your journey through FRAZZLED to FABULOUS!

## THE QUALITY OF YOUR COMMUNITY

**ONE OF THE** most valued gifts in my life HAS been my Royal Court…my treasured friends. Who you associate with does matter! You will discern who in your CIRCLE of friends will lift you in life, and who will tear you down. Once you know how you *read* and *respond* to people, it gets easier to recognize when someone who PUTS YOU DOWN will also BRING YOU DOWN. If you honestly want to move through FRAZZLED to FABULOUS, then it may be time to make a choice to separate yourself from the people who bring you down, suck the life out of you, and decrease your feelings of worth. It is also your choice to surround yourself with people who believe in you and support you.

Let me help you out here…do you have one special friend whom you know you can call or reach out to when you need one? It is easy for you to identify them, right? Well, imagine having an entire Royal Court of four or five friends just like that one amazing friend. Just imagine, you are surrounded by people who pick you up, support your dreams, and teach you a better, easier way to do life! This unique collection of friends includes people who help you look at what made you fall, analyze it and help you quickly get back on the road to success.

I happily share the secret success weapon I've learned works for me. It is at once complex, yet simple! For the last five years, I have said, "yes," to DOING LIFE in a big, non-negotiable way. To find the support I needed to do so consistently, I surrounded myself with an amazing and cherished group of caring, committed, extraordinary world-changers, who are an enormous blessing in my life.

I WAS playing small; however, these ladies loved me enough to break the chains that bound me as I hid out from bigger dreams. They encouraged me to STEP UP…to embrace and use the gift and talents God showers upon me…to help women move through FRAZZLED to FABULOUS and turn possibilities into realities.

Readers, STOP! and IMAGINE… the transformation that is possible when you accept the permission to surround yourself with people who will give you real feedback and teach you how you can show up and live your DREAM LIFE. No one should go it alone in life—NO ONE—and the quality of your tribe or royal court does matter! Also, creating a space, which protects you from negative people in your life is necessary. It initially may seem difficult; however, it will be worth it!

---

Make the choice to fill your life with people who believe in you and create boundaries or distance for those who don't. You won't regret it, I promise!

---

## YOUR DREAMS MATTER

*Each man should frame life so that at some future hour fact and his dreaming meet.*

~ Victor Hugo (1802 – 1885)

French poet, novelist, essayist, playwright, and dramatist of the Romantic movement.

**YOU WILL BE** happy to know there is no good reason to continue living a FRAZZLED life. However, it is critical to realize that if your dreams don't matter to YOU, then they will matter to NO ONE ELSE. When you think about the things you want from life and how you will achieve them, it's important to know there are two things in life over which you have one hundred percent control: your effort and your attitude, both of which are driven by your choices. You can CHOOSE to get up every day with joy and expect amazing opportunities to come your way or you can CHOOSE to be grumpy over what happened the day before that you had absolutely no control over. With this as the cornerstone of what I want to share next that impacts your ability to embrace your dreams, I invite you to look at three distinct areas of YOUR life.

**#1: Your Thoughts**: Bad thoughts tear you down, period! **WHO** you **ARE** starts from the inside out and if you constantly think, *I suck*, or, *I can't do this*, then guess what, you are one hundred percent right! It is part of the human experience to be what you think you are.

Unfortunately, those bad thoughts now become words.

**#2: Your Speech**: It has been proven that by your words you are justified, and you will become what you continue to say you are. As you think it in your heart and speak it with your mouth, you will become that!

Along the way, I discovered the better solution is to understand the relationship between your words and heart. Remember, Jesus said, "For a man's words will always express what has been treasured in his heart" (Luke 6:45). Once you understand how much your words are a mirror of your heart you can begin to measure the very essence of your character, simply by recording your words and listening to yourself. This process is not about how you feel, or how hard you try to convince yourself what a good person you are, but the natural utterances of your words.

---

*You see, death and life are in the power of your tongue.*

---

Think about this! Is it not likely the garbage you have in your life today is because of the rubbish you spoke about yesterday or the days or weeks before? Were you aware that words are containers, and they carry power?

I am compelled to ask again, "Are you ready?" Are you emotionally prepared to make a choice to change your thinking and choose to SPEAK GOOD into your life and future? When you choose good thoughts and begin to speak them, you will experience those thoughts and words becoming a reality. You get to CHOOSE!

## Create, Clarify, and Set Goals

**Nothing grounds you** so much in your move through FRAZZLED to FABULOUS like creating a roadmap for your goals. At a very young age, my Uncle Dan taught me, "Goals don't GET YOU ANYWHERE, Celeste; they TAKE YOU EVERYWHERE," and he was so right! His message has proven true many times over. I learned over the many years of my life the value of creating monthly and yearly goals and the importance of looking at them daily to celebrate the success of the ones I achieved. Add to that the wisdom to give me permission to make small adjustments to the ones I have not. I also attribute the benefits of goal setting to be a huge factor to why I have been so successful as I've persevered in life and slowly and steadily moved through FRAZZLED to FABULOUS time and time again.

## How to Create Goals.

**When I think** about setting goals, I consider it a plan to LIVE MY LIFE MY WAY! Unfortunately, far too many people feel they are rather adrift in life. They look back, seeing how hard they've worked, but feeling they have gotten nowhere worthwhile.

From personal experience, I feel the key reason people feel this way is from the lack of time spent thinking about what they want from life. They have not taken that time to formulate specific goals and as with any major journey, with no real idea of your destination, there is simply no way to know where you will arrive.

The process need not be complex or complicated. Make your goals simple. Consider a few I've had in my life; they reflect just how simple goals can be as you move through FRAZZLED to FABULOUS.

**Goal # 1:** Wake up with joy!

One of the favorite memories I have about my grandmother, whom we called Jai Jai, is how she got out of bed every day with great joy and expectation about what the day would bring. As soon as her feet hit the floor she would say,

---

*"Good morning, world. What amazing things do you have for me today?"*

---

She made the CHOICE to get up every day expecting great things. When I look back on her life and the joy and passion for life she woke up with every day, it was truly no surprise she had such an extraordinary life.

**Goal #2:** Read a motivating quote or book each morning:

Reading informs and inspires us. It is often the mainstay of my day and over the years I've developed a daily habit of reading five to ten scriptures and listening to a fifteen-minute mediation. I give full credit to this consistent daily action step for the strength I've needed myriad times to persevere and move through FRAZZLED to FABULOUS. One book I read daily, the Bible, reminds me of the many promises in the scriptures I shared with you. I cherish the many reminders that:

I can do all things through Christ who strengthens me.

All things work together for good regardless of the roadblocks that come our way.

I am more than a conqueror!

I am treasured...

I am beautiful...

I am loved.

Do you have a favorite book or several? If not, take the time to find a few, in which you can find the strength, confidence, and wisdom to create a roadmap to move you through FRAZZLED to FABULOUS.

**Goal #3:** Nutrition is an integral part of achieving all we desire in life. This has prompted me to eat three balanced small snacks throughout the day in addition to three healthy, high protein, low sugar meals. You are encouraged to consider the same path to healthy living; maybe it's time to give up soda pop or coffee or cut back fifty to seventy-five percent of your daily intake of it.

**Goal #4:** I realize the idea of scheduling probably doesn't make you want to break into song, but it is something we all must do so we can have a successful and fulfilling life. I have found a schedule helps me stay clear about my purpose.

---

*Our time is precious, and we should value how we spend it; if we don't decide what matters in advance, our time is wasted on things that don't move us through FRAZZLED to FABULOUS.*

---

If I don't stick to my schedule, I find myself *spinning wheels*! It becomes too easy to focus my time and energy on low-priority objectives or put others' priorities ahead of my own. Thus...I've committed to sticking to a daily schedule and the three things to which I am committed to getting done each day or week, which I am confident will move me through FRAZZLED to FABULOUS.

### WHAT DOES LIFE LOOK LIKE WITHOUT A GAME PLAN OR GOALS?

**WITHOUT A GAME** plan or goals to follow, you begin to feel like you are just going around in circles and not able to accomplish anything. Or possibly you start a project, and then another, and yet another, until you feel you complete nothing.

I have worked with hundreds of student-athletes and women over the last fifteen years who have made the choice to move through FRAZZLED to FABULOUS and have created amazing opportunities in their lives. They have learned to embrace their dreams and their why; they have set goals and now share their gifts and talents boldly with the world. I have watched peace and joy enter their lives abundantly because they have made the choice to live their dream life. Remember, God wants to take you through FRAZZLED to FABULOUS and create amazing opportunities in your life.

## ARE YOU READY?

*Action springs not from thought, but from a readiness for responsibility.*

~ G. M. Trevelyan (1876 – 1962)

English Author and Historian

**ARE YOU READY** to take the steps necessary to guide you to live your dream life?

Today I want to open you to the opportunity to work together because I want you to step into living your DREAM LIFE and move through FRAZZLED to FABULOUS. To do this, it is extremely important that you CHOOSE to:

set patterns of consistent actions each day,
wake up daily expecting amazing opportunities, and
give thanks for where you are.

NO ONE has to—nor should they have to—go this alone and via my mentorship program, I will walk you through the tools and strategies to move through FRAZZLED to FABULOUS time and time again. However, it must start with YOU and your WILLINGNESS to GO FOR IT and choose to live your BEST LIFE! You deserve to be blessed—not stressed, unfocused—not FRAZZLED.

I take a stand for you, and once again, I challenge you to create a game plan of what your dream life would look like and then GO FOR IT! It can be quite simple, really; it begins with believing in yourself and then taking DAILY action steps to turn your dreams into realities. You must ask yourself, "Am I ready to embrace my dreams and the life-changing impact they can CREATE for me?"

Eleanor Roosevelt once said, "The future belongs to those who BELIEVE IN the beauty OF THEIR DREAMS," and she is absolutely right!

I believe it is not by chance YOU read this book; I believe it is your time to be an overcomer and step into a lifestyle style that allows you to:

let go of perfection,
create healthy boundaries, and
positively persevere through life's struggles.

Please always remember that:

> *"You are beautifully and wonderfully made and that when God sees you, He sees his perfect child that He loves endlessly."*

Please do not allow Satan's lies to define you. Own your identity in Christ!

As a motivational speaker, Charleston Parker inspires, "In life, I have learned that you have three choices: to give in, to give up, or to give it all you've got." I feel the best choice, always, is to…

---

*Give it all you've got!*

---

# WHERE I AM MEANT TO BE

## EVEN IF PERHAPS ONLY FOR THIS MOMENT

Annmarie Gray

A FASCINATING WOMAN WHO HISTORICALLY HAS LOOKED LIFE FULL IN THE FACE AND MADE LIFE HAPPEN—MOSTLY ON HER TERMS!

**DESIGNING A LIFE** meant to be fulfilling and rewarding is an unending quest, and Annmarie embraces the reality that being outdoors feeds the soul.

Competing on various athletic teams during her youth, serving the public as a police officer for twenty years, contributing ten years to classroom instruction, and developing law enforcement leaders, has contributed to Annmarie's passion to influence others through curiosity and a healthy taste of excellence.

CHANGE could well be Annmarie's life word as she has learned to navigate change with confidence and passion while in the great OUTDOORS—her preferred venue. She has learned that experiencing the benefits of the outdoors can outweigh any fear or doubt that may filter in as daily dissatisfactions.

Annmarie is committed to contributing to society, freedom, and a bit of whimsy every day. This commitment leads to her ability to connect with, encourage, and develop the willingness of others to recognize change as a natural occurrence in life. Her enthusiasm and understanding of brain science elevates her expertise in coaching and encouraging exploration into what is next—while living in the now.

Annmarie's greatest gift to life is her ability to connect individuals, teams (small and large), and organizations to strategies that successfully regulate stress and fear while piloting change.

Change in mindset...

Change in lifestyle...

Change in work-life...

Change in organizational structure.

Through creating a work-life balance lifestyle, clients depend on Annmarie's support to help them recognize and embrace the possibilities and trust themselves in the face of uncertainty, growing pains, and accompanying discomfort.

ARE YOU READY?

Those who know Annmarie agree she has never met a stranger, yet she keeps environments safe while moving the needle toward change. Resounding outcomes working with Annmarie include increased community, connection, and trust.

Annmarie Gray
Matters of Gray
annmarie@mattersofgray.com
310.345.0065

# WHERE I AM MEANT TO BE

EVEN IF PERHAPS ONLY FOR THIS MOMENT

---

*Attitude is a CHOICE.*
*Optimism is a CHOICE;*
*Giving is a CHOICE.*
*Respect is a CHOICE.*
*Whatever CHOICE you make*
*makes you.*
*Choose wisely.*

---

**LIFE FOR ME** has been a series of changes and transitions. I have learned to endure transition, each leading to something, someone, someplace new. MY CHOICE!

My professional life began with pinball machine repair, designing a pathway of bumps, bruises, job descriptions, and colleagues, culminating in a celebratory departure from a twenty-year career in law enforcement. My home life has also taken a few serpentine turns—from sibling to roommate…to wife to single woman forging her own path…on to single parenting, single motherhood, and living alone again, naturally!

Over time, I discovered that identifying what brings me joy and pleasure is as crucial in life as identifying what *does not*. A good part of my life has been spent defining optimal experiences, making changes by running, by standing still, finally to CHOOSING. Not always ideal.

As you read through the *chapters of my life*, I encourage you to embrace both my vulnerability and my courage. It has been a journey in and of itself…braving what it took to face myself at times, and to share bits of the roller-coaster ups and downs that kept life, well, interesting!

## CHAPTERS OF MY LIFE

*Destinations are endpoints. Journeys are learnings, paths of possibilities, blossoming…fresh beginnings.*

~ RASHEED OGUNLARU (1970 - )
LONDON-BASED LIFE, BUSINESS, AND
CORPORATE COACH.

**THROUGHOUT THESE** pages, you will read about the various elements of a formula that has defined and outlined my willingness and excitement to endure change…several undeniable methods driving transition and change, which have lent to the freedom of my journey(s). I distinguish CHANGE (something that happens to me) from TRANSITION (something I cause to occur). As you read my story, perhaps you will discover distinct evidence of your experiences of change—or your desire to do so.

### PROVOKING THOUGHTS…

Are you frightened of change?
Do you resist change?

When dissatisfied, do you take action or does the action take you?

My life has been a revolving door of each. All ultimately resulting in emotional well-being and a willingness to take responsibility—or perhaps garnering a bit of each. Timing, circumstances, and community have dictated my every reaction or response.

---

*It is important to profess that my spectacular life looks different every day!*

---

There were days I felt hopeless, trapped, left without a choice. My younger years were riddled with expectations and any reference to change was negative. Today I recognize that changing is not quitting, giving up, or even a sign of lacking confidence. Changing employment too soon appeared I was not a reliable employee; was I a quitter? Leaving a job because it did not suit me left a taste of giving up; leaving something I did not excel in pointed to a lack of confidence. Moving from city to city represented running from—not necessarily running to. This recognition is evidenced by myriad reasons, strategies, and approaches to implementing change. Feeling uninspired, a common prompt for change in my life, was like a prison sentence. What will others think if I move again?

Will I ever find what I am meant to do?

Why do I get restless so easily?

A most significant concern came when I was nearly refused an appointment to the police department. The primary obstacle was if my husband were to return, I would leave the job to reconcile with him. Today, fortunately for me, inspiration is everywhere. Just look around!

When you are hit hard in the heart and feel uninspired, might I suggest you stop and reach out to someone—a friend, a colleague, a family member, even a stranger! Seek insights through sharing ideas. Perhaps reaching more deeply into yourself will lead to an inspired solution. Through several of my own life transitions, decisions and choices were mine alone. Because I lacked self-confidence, I frequently felt the fear of hearing my decision was ill-advised or considered a possible failure…each proved an obstacle to my willingness to share. More recently, however, being accompanied by deep friendships and connections has altered this perspective.

Trust me, this life is not meant to be a walk you take alone—when you go inside yourself, your head specifically, you are typically taken to a deep and dark place. Have faith in my shared experiences as I gently encourage you to seek community—a community of partnership that is sure to add confidence and laughter to your circle.

---

*Life, for me, has proven to be a training ground for possibility. A training ground navigating change in varied patterns.*

---

Life provides many provoking thoughts and how we perceive them predicates many of our life choices as we assess whether they are:

Intentional

Unplanned

My idea vs. your idea

Someone else's idea

Inevitable

There are subsets of each. Some life-altering; some I often refer to as earth-shattering; others benign or simply nice.

Viktor Frankl in his book, *Man's Search for Meaning,* outlines purpose as "motivation for living." The age-old question: "Why am I here?" comes to mind. When CHOICES ARE MADE FOR ME, because I hesitate or fear choosing—my choice dissipates and ultimately minimizes the power of my purpose. I call this CHASING. Alternatively, when I STEP INTO AN IDEA or a possibility, I am powerfully CHOOSING

---

*Do you wish to choose your circumstances or chase them?*

---

This distinction of CHOOSING OR CHASING has elevated an awareness for me in most decisions I make today. Choices as simple as travel plans, social invitations, developing partnerships. Choices as convoluted as accepting a contract, creating partnerships, taking on professional opportunities. Recently, I was introduced to my human design. My individual design suggests I feel an immediate gut response of YES or NO. Following this model has strengthened my resolve and minimized the chase which had been a chronic experience for me.

Regardless of which change or TRANSITION you may be enduring at any time, the lyrics of *Chapters of My Life,* written by Brett Young, Gavin DeGraw, and Scott Copperman, say it all for me.

*There's no perfect life, you can't hold back time*
*But you hold on tight, hopin' you might find*
*Every page you turn is a lesson learned*
*Ain't we all, ain't we all just tryna get it right?*

**IF REACHING OUT** to someone does not do it for you, embrace the challenge to change your physiology! Early on, I discovered a simple practice that unlocks a less inspiring temperament to one of appreciation and joy. This practice supports choosing something more appealing to your sensibilities. I found when I stay stuck in these unpleasant moods, far too many decisions are MADE FOR ME—which subsequently takes me out of the CHOOSING zone and slams me right into the CHASING zone.

---

*Some who know me might say I have never met a stranger.*

---

There are many benefits when connecting with strangers—with all humans—with all living things. Benefits, which envelope all parties, even when resistance is at play.

A-simple, immediate strategy perpetuates my practice of reaching out to strangers. This practice has followed me throughout my adult life, with associates and strangers alike.

This STRANGER ENGAGEMENT feeds me!

In my early twenties, as a marathon runner, I ran around the reservoir in Central Park during the early mornings. I made a game of speaking to others running or walking, counting the number of people who responded to my greeting, and those who did not. I truly enjoyed the experience of those who did respond and felt a slight disappointment over those who did not. While studying brain science many years later, I recognized what was happening to cause such happy feelings. Recently, some forty years later, while in Chicago, I walked down Michigan Avenue late morning with a friend and lifelong resident of Chicago. I greeted passersby!

He was shocked by this and laughs about it whenever we are together. He shares the story with others…an amazing surprise in his voice. "People don't do that!" he exclaims after telling the story. I find this comical because I still feel that same joy today as I did in 1980s NYC. It is science! Our brain is always listening! Whenever a stranger does address me, all nature of feel-good chemicals surge through my body, flooding me with joy, inspiration, happiness—it shifts my physiology in an instant. I deliberately CHOOSE these momentary surges of connection! I also CHOOSE to inspire these momentary surges of joy and encouragement in others whenever an opportunity presents itself. Frankly, this feeds my commitment to contribution.

Try it, you might like it!

Each originating from my brain, these rapid and effective momentary adjustments have led me to bravely explore change through a simple framework. One that has smoothed the wrinkled edges of CHOICE and frequently proves successful for me.

Intentional—Change that is planned.

Unplanned—Life-altering change that is unintended, sometimes scary.

Inevitable—Temporary, get me out of here change.

Collaborative—My idea, your idea, our idea

I can now accept that everyone's reference for living is different, but I want you to know that you, too, can experience such inoculation anytime…through the kind of experiences that are invigorating for me.

---

*I look at change as a different moment snuggled into the daily grind called life. Without embracing change, I might simply identify life as mere existence.*

---

A specific purpose typically drives choices—choices that identify our specifically designed purpose comes naturally for some yet remain unclear for others. In reality, my purpose eluded me for what felt a very long lifetime, shifting quite frequently. For years, I felt tremendous overwhelm and envy for those who appeared to know their specific direction and live their best life, with what appeared to be ease. This sense of frustration consumed me more than once, specifically when speaking with a dear woman I was fortunate to call a friend. She was the owner of a local, progressive, and innovative preschool. She had an uncanny ability to explore from love and caring and I found in her a safe haven during darker days when I was still unaware of the value of exploration. Our conversations highlighted my longing to have it all! CRAZY MAKING as I had no idea what IT ALL truly meant.

During my short-lived marriage, our life was quite elaborate. We travelled, we partied, we owned and operated a restaurant and bar in Washington DC; we focused on fitness while indulging in unhealthy practices. Money, or lack of thereof, never appeared to be a deterrent. An observer might have said I already had IT ALL, yet that lifestyle did not serve me. You might say, "You were CHASING a life rather than CHOOSING to live your life!"

In retrospect, the beauty of it all is how my purpose has materialized in many forms.

---

*Each experience led me here—to NOW!*
*Precisely where I feel* **I am meant to be!**
*Even if perhaps only for this moment.*

---

## I AM THE POWERFUL MISTRESS OF TRANSITION!

**CHANGE INVIGORATES ME.** Through my several iterations of Annmarie Gray, life's lessons have been riddled with a cacophony of joy, fear, excitement, depression. Even loneliness. Self-doubt, clearly lined with financial setbacks, has since transformed into a deep appreciation for each experience and its associated lesson. The following brief overview of my experiences tell their own story of my life changes.

### COLLEGE YEARS:

Disneyland ride operator.

Supper club cocktails and food…and where I met my husband,

Retail shop: fashion showroom rep and model.

Simultaneously holding two or three jobs served as my social outlet.

### MARRIED YEARS:

Pursued, unsuccessfully I might add, a lifelong dream career as a flight attendant. One of my dreams as a young girl was to become a stewardess and my older brother a pilot. He became the pilot; I never did get the flight attendant position.

Fashion industry: showroom salesperson, model, executive assistant to the president of one of the first discount designer retail companies.

I also enjoyed competing as a bodybuilder, ran marathons, enlisted in various racquetball tournaments, and coached high school athletics

### POST MARRIAGE SPLIT UP:

I moved to NYC and found my way back to the fashion industry.

I returned to California and spent my time in table service, college courses, personal training, squash and racquetball, police work.

I currently reside in Nashville, Tennessee.

Suffice it to say, I am quite comfortable with change. Revisiting the previously mentioned framework, I now recognize how many of them were TRANSITIONS rather than CHANGES. Of course, much emotional turmoil and fear drove these shifts. Mostly, joy and kindness remained constant throughout each of these life experiences. Some were planned, several unplanned, a few inevitable, and the more recent…collaborative.

Self-acceptance now replaces the judgment and personal need to fulfill another's beliefs of what is best for me, although self-doubt does continue to sneak in now and then. The current difference is that I more quickly recognize the influence I have over falling victim to such unproductive emotion. Tools have been made available to me…all through the willingness to look at myself and take responsibility for my own growth and personal choices

---

*My life took a turn for the better when I became willing to recognize and believe, we teach people how to treat us.*

---

A common practice for me was to tell people what I believed they wanted to hear. To save face, to lie and to fake life became my persona. To accept responsibility was often difficult for me; worrying about others' opinions kept me from living true even to myself. My whimsical approach to life was uncomfortable for those who loved me. They worried about my future, my financial stability, my single lifestyle—at least that was my impression. I allowed teasing and judgment, feeling like I didn't measure up, or staying in unsatisfying situations to become common practice. I went so far as to adopt the practice of teasing myself, perhaps to minimize others' opportunity to do so first. Everyone likely knew…everyone but me, that is!

Blame and accusation tend to be a strategy for many who are not satisfied with situations they find themselves in. When we CHOOSE for ourselves and make decisions to support our choices, responsibility is placed right where it belongs. When I finally got that lesson, my life became much more fulfilling; much more REAL! Becoming accountable has changed everything for me—my life is now one of my own CHOOSING. It took a while to teach people how to treat me differently and I continue to be a work in progress. In fact, teaching MYSELF how to treat ME also continues to be a journey.

The most profound reality is that our brain is always listening. We create reality by speaking it aloud or even thinking it…self-talk being extremely powerful!

---

*MY journey of change has led me to learn how to treat myself.*
*How to embrace my own choices.*

---

This has been and remains a challenging feat and I caution you to not kid yourself! The neuropathways of self-doubt, self-sabotage, and whatever *self*-concerns drive our life paths still rear their ugly heads, as our brain is always listening.

As you read on, you will likely key in on the similarities and variances between each account in this anthology. You will find that when you live in the FRAZZLED, transitioning to FABULOUS often proves repetitious. First, you must ground yourself in what transition means to you. Again, for me, a transition is an intentional act. For me, exhilarating defines transition; change becomes my word for habit. So, buckle up, put your feet up, embrace the possibilities!

Yes, that is me! They (possibilities) are endless, and if you look around, you will find inspiration is everywhere! During your journey of moving through Frazzled to Fabulous, you are invited to courageously seek out inspiring experiences that might transform your energy, moment by moment! As you read this powerful collection of stories, be attentive to moments in which you might recognize yourself.

Yes, FABULOUS is a choice, as is FRAZZLED. To accept each moment as a minute-by-minute temporary state, and purposefully shift your mindset, is certain to induce your brain to surge with the appropriate chemicals to drive the emotions you desire…the intended outcomes in your best interest.

## CHOOSING IS A DISTINCTION.

**THROUGH THE JUGGERNAUT** of transitions, a realization dawned on me that has been a stronghold in each aspect of my life: living, laughing, coaching, teaching; even crying. Much of my life has been spent CHASING. My eyes have widened to the reality of how much time I spent chasing a life others believed appropriate for me, rather than CHOOSING a life.

MY LIFE!

Shannon King, a co-author of this anthology, and a very dear friend and colleague, shared with me my HUMAN DESIGN. The clarity this system provided opened me to a freedom I had not previously experienced. HUMAN DESIGN, by the way, is a system that reveals the person you were born to be and the life you were meant to live. This has truly impacted the way I live and how I see myself fitting in this vast and wondrous world.

I discovered I am a Generator!

I learned the invaluable understanding that my life force is motivated by change. I am DESIGNED to embrace change…to experience the fulfilled life I have aspired to throughout my lifetime. Accepting this nuance and living into it has freed me to not only thrive but to guide others in how to treat me to serve my highest and best purpose.

---

*The life I now experience is* ***appropriate*** *for me.*

---

Today, I recognize, embrace, live, and share my life as a mature and confident woman. *Ok, most of the time.* Clearly, life for me has shifted dramatically. CHASING represents a kind of desperation to me now, but of course, chasing remains some part of my journey. My brain is always listening. I've discovered that to become lifelong friends with your brain is a most valuable life skill and accompanying this friendship with my brain is a passion for learning.

Living the American Dream fed my psyche from an early age. Imagining what that dream was kept me hungry yet baffled. Hungry in the way a teething baby might experience the joy and curiosity of chewing on an unrecognizable object that felt smooth, cold, and soothing. Why not explore in every way possible? Baffled because even today, true satisfaction often seems to REMAIN an arm's reach away. I say (write) this, not as a bad thing. Simply as a reality I've come to accept.

As a young athlete, chasing served as a winning recipe—I was competitive, coordinated, driven, and a very strong, skilled athlete. I shone on the field and on the court. I even excelled on the neighborhood streets with my brothers and our neighborhood kids. For several reasons, that competitive edge was less attractive and not quite as powerful in my workplace and just as often—not in my social settings.

Despite this obstacle, my JOY AND WHIMSY FOR LIVING was another winning formula throughout all endeavors. Until recently, I found it difficult to recall what drove my being upset. My memory for misery is short, while joy and whimsy prevail. Not surprisingly, people found me engaging, which I better understand today, knowing how our brain responds to stimuli. A common reference to me, mostly in the law enforcement arena, was that I was *too nice*. Fortunately, this personal trait did not overcome my persona through twenty-plus years on the police force.

During my days in policing, a general assumption was that females were softer and nicer, while male officers were tough and gruff. Not surprisingly, fellow officers would routinely request my assistance when dealing with difficult people who were not destined for jail. I had the patience with which they chose not to engage. Female officers were often dispatched to sexual assaults, neighbor disputes, baby-in-distress calls.

I recall returning to work following the birth of my daughter. The first two weeks I was dispatched to several baby-in-distress calls. Each seemed to feed an unbearable vulnerability in me…clearly a result that was not intentioned.

One event that consumed me for too many years involved a shooting. I was asked about my actions and immediately presented evidence of my tactics. This inquiry occurred while I stood in the middle of the street, alone, thinking about my seven-month-old daughter who was at home with a caregiver. I remember the event like it was yesterday, the questions and doubt, *What am I doing in this situation?*

As a sergeant, I was diligent in encouraging officers to step away if they felt themselves getting agitated with a subject, which I knew was a common occurrence from the personal experience of sitting with subjects awaiting medical clearance. I made the offer to radio me for assistance; I was happy to remove them from any potential misconduct, even if verbal. I had no skin in the game; my ego was not being challenged. The offer was accepted on many occasions.

Three officers I supervised happened upon me one late night, as I dealt with a belligerent pedestrian on an outdoor shopping mall sidewalk. Sensing I was getting progressively more agitated; each of them carefully approached me from behind. One intervened with the pedestrian, the other two, grasping an elbow, escorted me away, safeguarding my potential misconduct. No good deed goes unpunished…they were my saving grace that night! Even though we now see each other infrequently, we still chuckle about the night they saved my proverbial bacon. Ironically, today's policing efforts REQUIRE interactions that are approachable, kind, nice. I consider I was living ahead of the time, being innovative, practicing tenets of procedural justice long before the phrase was coined. It was something that I acknowledged as being different or too nice; I was insightful, service driven, empathetic. Even so, I have been known to *bury nice* when I feel confronted. I'm still working on that one!

As the neighborhood kid on the block who competed for competition and recreation, I perfectly represented the intentional change spoken of earlier. I excelled at what I enjoyed, fit in because

I made it fun for everyone, walked away each day feeling satisfied and fulfilled. AND IT WAS MY CHOICE!

Fortunately, later in life that neighborhood kid made a transition; the clarity between CHOOSING or CHASING came into being and shifted me to embrace a healthier mindset. Ironically, I have been blessed with the RESILIENCE TO SUSTAIN A LIFE OF CHANGE. The unplanned, unanticipated, and sometimes unrealistic choices—to many who knew and loved me—were considered to be unquestionably ill-advised choices. In retrospect, however, each change promoted growth. Wisdom. Personal satisfaction. Not to mention worry, doubt, and unsolicited advice from loved ones. I understand that risk-taking is not for everyone. My perspective was not about risk—I was chasing a dream, not taking chances. True confessions: my confidence in these actions was often riddled with fear and doubt until I knew that everything worked out.

---

*I choose the dream. I thrive in change.*

---

There was a day all I wanted was to be over the moon happy. Contentment sounded dreadful to the *young* Annmarie. When I say young, I confess I still considered forty-plus young.

Outlining a framework for my life began when I was able to engage with authenticity, self-acceptance, and faith. When I combine these characteristics, perhaps labeled strengths, into my life's purpose, the fog lifts—making my life, and WHAT'S NEXT, clear to me.

I am committed to contribution, freedom, and a bit of whimsy every day. However, before identifying these *life principles*, the living I had become familiar with was driven by dreaming, desiring, and yet…dismissing myself in any equation of possibilities.

I still dream and am filled with desire…they remain, yet I no longer dismiss possibilities. Oh, no! I've shifted to creating opportunities and designing adventures because I understand just how opportunities inspire me as potential adventures.

## We're All in the Same Boat

*We are all in the same boat, in a stormy sea, and we owe each other a terrible loyalty.*

~ Gilbert Keith Chesterton (1874 – 1936)

English writer, philosopher, lay - theologian, and literary and art critic.

**Whether your boat** is in rough water or clear sailing; the skies are dumping with rain or sunny and clear; salt water, fresh water; sharks or minnows—we are all in the same metaphorical boat! Crafting a vessel to carry me through life is up to me. CHOOSING how to navigate the seas can be much more inspiring than fighting choppy waters others might see before me. Others' fears for me frequently minimize the adventure called my life. Just the same, on a large or small scale, whichever decision I arrive at is a CHOICE. And the reality remains: fear is a liar!

The Zac Brown Band, in a recently released song titled "Same Boat" sings:

*We all been kicked and knocked around*
*But you ain't gonna keep a good man down*

*You can run like hell from your mistakes*
*But you can't hide from your truth*

I've been seeking *my truth* for a good long time. Experience has shown one absolute: when something is right for me, or something does not fit, I innately know it immediately—with absolute certainty. Why then has it taken so much hesitation and deliberation, to align with any personal discovery? How have I become amenable to what other people choose for me?

---

*Is there a distinction between changing your mind and changing your life circumstance?*

---

Recently, unloading a storage unit here in Nashville, Tennessee, memories swirled in my brain. Emotions stopped me in my tracks. Evidence of several moves or relocations flooded my heart, my mind, my emotions. Joy and sadness embroiled me in curiosity. *Why did I save this? How can I get rid of this? What is it I am looking for with this move?* This particular clearing, unlike most, included long forgotten, moments from my PAST, accompanied by never experienced remnants of my daughter's relocations. Still reeling from the worldwide COVID-19 pandemic, which brought my adult daughter to stay with me BRIEFLY, incited so many more emotions than just the transition of my past.

While in the storage shed sorting, the methodology of my many relocations ignited my curiosity. *What prompted the many relocations?* Several were unplanned, thus messy, and scary. *Was I running from something? Did I truly see something better from the move? Was this move my idea?* Typically, yes. *If so, why?* For certain, on REFLECTION, each worked out. Unfortunately, each was a drain on my finances; each had someone expressing concern for me or suggesting I was being...well, you name the adjective!

With great interest, each move took me from one community and catapulted me to yet another, wherein I discovered I, unfortunately, have not been the most communicative with people who were dear friends. This trait caused fractures in relationships, which has required intervention to re-establish friendships. I still have work to do—hurt to remedy—at least I believe that to be true.

I AM LIKABLE AFTER ALL!

I cannot say with confidence that all breaches of these valuable relationships were intentional. By intentional, I reference the outcomes or circumstances, which now present themselves as examples of CHASING rather than CHOOSING whatever was to come.

Before transitioning to the role of mom, life was a series of jobs, adventures, missteps. They were not missteps of any critical consequence I recognized—but CHASING what felt was right. I received and passed on many opportunities. I still question if such squandering was due to self-doubt and fear. *Was I simply uncertain or was it unadulterated dissatisfaction?* In any event, opportunities do not always lead to fulfillment. And, if the passed over or missed opportunities lessened my efficacy and joy through life, I am not aware of such loss.

That leaves me with questions…lifelong questions. *Who am I? what do I want?* Recently, during a coaching conversation with a new colleague, turned friend, a distinction surfaced. Truth is, he pointed it out to me when he observed, "You speak more of what you don't want rather than what you really do desire."

His remark was quite a shock, yet I immediately noticed it to be true. More curious was how easily I notice this behavior in my clients and coach them into and through a mindset shift!

Fortunately, my awareness of this practice opened a door to shift my own well-entrenched habit. Now, when I take time to frame conversations around what I do want, my consciousness is dramatically illuminated, and doors to more impactful choices open for me.

### PROVOKING THOUGHTS...

What opportunities are right there for you to seize?

Are they worthy of pondering?

What steps do you take to ponder the possibilities?

How might your life experience be different?

My concerns and life experiences revolved around what Annmarie wanted—literally, that is until this little bundle of joy, responsibility, life force, was placed on my chest immediately following her birth. The overwhelm of "how do I do this" remains one of my most significant, life-altering realizations—a force unmatched by any other! Clearly, every woman reading this, who has given birth, recognizes the magnitude of this moment. Parenting partners are also, likely profoundly affected by this moment.

*"Everyone thinks about changing the world no one thinks about changing themselves."*

~ LEO TOLSTOY (1828 – 1910)
RUSSIAN WRITER.

**HAVING BEEN A** single woman for a very long time, this motherhood transition at thirty-seven introduced me to the unpredictable, unplanned journey we understand to be parenting. A most overwhelming privilege! Becoming a mother was and is still the most indelible and meaningful transition of my lifetime. Yet I repeat...an unplanned one. Before motherhood, aside from years of a marriage that ended in divorce...the concepts of CONSTANT and LIFELONG COMMITMENT were not in my lexicon. Ironically, recently having completed my probationary first year as a police officer, I appeared in a recruiting video stating, "This time is the first in my life I know where I will be five years from now!" I find that laughable today.

Previously averse to planning, it is presently more bearable. Until now, the most planning I had done was for Morgan's arrival. Fearing the financial demands, being both excited and terrified to be a mom, experiencing a change in assignment with the police department, and choosing a birthing partner were the most planning in which I recall engaging. Thirty years later, I am proud and pleased to say it all worked out.

---

*From my perspective, my daughter and I have a solid relationship riddled with love, mutual respect, laughter, disagreement, frustration...similar, I suppose, to most other family units.*

---

Back to the Nashville storage unit! These moments of housecleaning highlighted CHANGE in a way I had not examined before. There, in the quiet around me, I focused on myriad strategies to trace CHANGE and TRANSITION. Many people speak of disliking, even hating, change. Those moments in the Nashville storage unit stirred emotions around my most recent move.

This TRANSITION...I'd not considered beforehand how disruptive it might be for Morgan. During her stay with me, I began a remodel of my thousand-square-foot condo. It was a TRANSITION

I had been exploring and wishing to occur for quite a while. It happens that the opportunity presented itself and I said, "Yes!"

Morgan moved from the guest room into the master. The guest room, which was to become an extension of a great room, was where the construction would occur. I moved in there, which for me was a magnanimous gesture. Everything should be peachy, right? Well, not so much! The disruption in both of our lives had a topsy-turvy impact on anything it could possibly affect. Morgan had endured so much change and unpredictability—all of it was imposed upon her—none her choice. Most of all. living with her mother after being on her own for ten plus years. And in Nashville, of all places! Now, she suffered all because her mom imposed such disruption, without first examining the possible downsides. We did, however, survive the turmoil.

Morgan has since opted to stay in Nashville, in her own apartment, and has built what appears to be a life that serves her well. All turned out well with us, at least as I see it. Except, of course, the relief I knew she felt to be returning to her own life and is likely content to see me now and then—once in a while. To be honest, I've also realized I am not overly sad about having my own space back either.

---

*The way and the purpose for engaging in change vary with each experience. Planned, unplanned, purposeful, impetuous, scary, emotional, benign, and unimportant. All are a natural progression for me.*

---

This experience, and probably many others I never before reflected on, led me to a significant question, which I now greatly value, "Who else will this change impact?" An awareness has developed in my practices today to include other people's experiences and how my actions impact them. Sadly, for decades, my life followed a path of *what's in it for me* far more frequently than I feel comfortable admitting. Never intentionally, often unconsciously. Writing these chapters has highlighted my past behavior in a very profound way. The more I find clarity, the more it continues to unveil clouded memories and makes way for a deeper understanding of WHAT'S NEXT. As I experienced the blending of belongings and the obvious nature of our differences, my daughter, again, in an unexpected way, became the flashlight illuminating my affinity for newness and change. Truly, for life itself!

### PROVOKING THOUGHTS...

> *When unsettled, do you embrace change?*
>
> *What emotions invigorate you and which stop you in your tracks?*
>
> *Are you running away or running to?*
>
> *Most significant to me at this very moment was how preparing for transition has occurred throughout my life!*

Remember, I am not a planner. When the urge for some TRANSITION strikes, WHAT'S NEXT overtakes every bone in my body. Examining this from today's perspective prompts a more obvious excitement for what is next. Honestly looking inside, allowing myself to feel and face my life from the rearview mirror ignited roaring curiosity around my perspective of CHANGE and TRANSITION.

With each recognizable transition has come to a deeper sense of self-acceptance, although I'm still riddled with self-doubt—excitement peppered with fear. Mostly comes the realization that anything is possible, that I matter, and that I innately value people. When risk, determination, and trust accompany a decision to take that first step, my willingness is fortified to take it. My aim is for contribution, freedom, and a bit of whimsy every day!

*"Design the life you want to live, not the one that's been designed for you. You can take something and change it to what you need it to be" You don't necessarily have to go anywhere else to get it."*

~ RON FINLEY - RON FINLEY PROJECT
A REBEL WITH A GREEN THUMB.

## MY PATH TO ENDURING, EMBRACING, AND ENGAGING IN CHANGE

*The only way to make sense out of change is to plunge into it, move with it, and join the dance.*

Alan Wilson Watts (1915 – 1973)

British philosopher, writer, and speaker, best known as an interpreter, popularizing Eastern philosophy for a Western audience.

**CHOOSING TO CHANGE** my life circumstances was prompted by comparison. My quest to be different stemmed from childhood family experiences. One of nine siblings, the middle girl of three, provoked me to curiosity, rebellion, and a desperation to get out!

---

*I knew I was loved.*
*I knew I had talent.*
*I knew I was different.*

---

Unfortunately, being different was not necessarily safe for me. Teasing became a reality in my life, and I can attest to the reality that teasing is NOT a form of affection. I lived inside a world where being teased meant I fit in, from which I adopted a belief that being all the following—funny, kind, pretty, talented, and smart—was too great for any one female to handle. These were a combination of traits allowable for males. Females were wise to possess one or two, but heaven forbid, not all of them!

*"There's no conceit in our family,*
*she has it all!"*

~ Barbara Gray
My mother

This quote I heard from my mother at a moment when I was feeling my oats (feel one's oats: to act frisky or lively). In case you are curious, this saying, with its analogy to a horse that is lively after being fed, is American in origin and dates from the early nineteenth century.

My mother's comment, then, defined much of my freedom in behavior, instilling a bit of uncertain arrogance throughout my developing years. Although I'm not certain how the arrogance actually served me, I can attest to times it safeguarded my resolve.

Now, with the privilege to look back at my life through my aging lens, I nourish a level of curiosity often previously avoided, because reflecting on my life prompted a pain of which I was acutely aware but could not make sense of.

Claiming a path through FRAZZLED to FABULOUS stands today as one of the more significant invitations I have accepted in my lifetime. Finding myself in this community of women feeds my soul! Presented the opportunity to contribute to this anthology by sharing aspects of my journey solidified my sense of belonging and supports my commitment to contribution.

It has also occurred to me that what we SEE in others is rarely what is true of that person. My life framework is an effective, invigorating, and inspiring method for crafting FABULOUS simply by making shifts in circumstance, mindset, community, and even life choices. The overwhelming societal dislike of CHANGE has always baffled me. Perhaps the more effective strategy for me is addressing mindset. After all, our brain is always listening; it is a powerful ally and comprises pathways created and changed simply by CHOOSING.

---

*Maybe, a simple shift in mindset and language, adopting the word transition, eliminating the potentially negative connotation of change just may encourage a new way of unlocking possibilities.*

---

You see, behavior and personal engagement are contagious. Have you noticed how the attitude of those surrounding you forms a blanket of emotion, which mirrors the same in you? Being fascinated with the study of the human brain has made everything I do some type of contribution to society. Lofty, yes? Yet quite simple.

You may have surmised my need for independence simply from what you've read thus far. My family was the primary source of community for me throughout my early years. Seeking agreement and acceptance from members of my family was important. Ill-advised? Perhaps. A challenge stemming from these early experiences is that my approach to life, my true nature differs greatly from my family members. Specifically, those with whom I have built a social life.

---

*I typically do not play it safe.*
*My approach to life and to choices is bent more toward the energy and excitement found in abandon and freedom.*

---

My family is nurturing and loving; I believe that to be their intention anyway. Believing this to be true much of my life endorsed a practice of allowing others to direct me in what they considered the best way for me to live my life. Seeking approval, questioning my own ability, and making decisions aligned with others' opinions over time became a less than effective and dissatisfying practice. I do feel loved by my family. Unfortunately, I do not experience their confidence in my choices. They are, however, concerned for me, of that I am certain.

Lacking that familial confidence led me down a path of craving acceptance, which became a deep-seated and perhaps unhealthy trait. A trait, which diminished my ability to embrace self-acceptance. In fact, the many elements that develop a strong sense of self eluded me, until I moved to Nashville, where I attended a women's conference, and purposefully sought a community of acceptance, contribution, and friendship.

# NOTICEABLE LIFE-ALTERING EVENTS

*Life is a series of natural and spontaneous changes. Don't resist them - that only creates sorrow. Let reality be reality. Let things flow naturally forward in whatever way they like.*

~Lao Tzu (571 BC)

Ancient Chinese philosopher and writer.

**I HAVE LIVED** in many places, worked in several industries, experienced moderate to notable successes, felt respect, and felt loved. Yet...I was unhappy and could not see why. Three of the many life-altering events speak loudly enough to my affinity and capacity to thrive in the face of change; they are being shared here. Perhaps through these few stories, you will gain a better understanding of the power and potential CHANGE and/or TRANSITION afford.

## 1972: WHITTIER, CALIFORNIA – COLLEGE BOUND

OR NOT!

At seventeen, I was an accomplished athlete, engaged to be married, and had just learned I was awarded an athletic scholarship to college. Some of the first scholarships that resulted from the newly adopted Title VIIII, which provided female athletes a benefit previously only offered to male students. These early scholarships included classes exclusively. Equipment, housing, and incidentals were not included.

Dad and I discussed accepting the scholarship. Who would have thought such a basic conversation would significantly change the course of my life? All I wanted was to become a professor AND an athletic coach (I dreamt of American basketball player and coach Pat Summit's life). Dad said he and mom could not afford to send me to college, but they wanted me to get an education so if anything happened to my husband, I could take care of my kids. My memories fail me as to my reasoning those many years ago, but guess who rebelled and turned down the opportunities to attend college on scholarship?

In retrospect, this rash decision may have been my inaugural step into designing a life I CHOSE to live. Was this a CHOICE or was it a CHASE? I fearlessly identify this TRANSITION as unplanned—MY IDEA!

---

*Were I to label anything in my life as a regret, this is most assuredly THE EVENT!*

---

A motto stands, by which I've lived since Morgan was five years old, "Destined to be an old woman with no regrets." Today, I simply try to be more intentional and selective with my choices.

## 1978: Marina del Rey, California—Walking Down the Aisle

**Life finds me** a twenty-three-year-old, enamored by love and designing a life I so wish to live. Bill and I dated for about a year and opted to marry during the Christmas Holiday. We wisely thought better about eloping, we CHOSE instead to plan an intimate wedding for February 18th in our small apartment, surrounded by family and friends. Not surprisingly, my father refused to give me away as we were not marrying in the Catholic Church. Even less so, Mom asked me if I was pregnant because we were moving so quickly.

The day of the ceremony provided memories I would not have expected. The minister asked to repeat after him, "I, Bill." It was me who repeated, "I, Bill!" Who was nervous? Bill's dearest friend hollered out, "She is beautiful—no one ever said she was smart." My tension lightened, as everyone laughed. However, it was not until the moment in which I committed this story to paper that I recognized the insidious nature of this teasing. There seemed to be no limitations…no filters of humanity.

Bill, my twin brother, congratulated Bill, my husband, and asked that he take good care of me. My new husband retorted, "Are you kidding, she is going to take care of me!"

There were two toppers on the cake; Bill designed our wedding cake—chocolate with drunk pink elephants falling off the sides; We slept on the floor in our den while his parents slept in our bed. Looking back on the collective of these events, it is little wonder I questioned the formula for a long-standing, successful marriage!

We moved to Washington, DC, built a social circle which ultimately brought us to remodeling and opening a restaurant and bar, became involved in some unsavory business practices, and separated in 1981, after which I moved to New York City. After a failed attempt to make our relationship work, our divorce followed in June 1984.

This series of events fits nicely into the category of self-acceptance and CHOOSING a life more suited to my own design. Not my idea, inevitable, life-altering.

A tremendous positive note around my marriage came from two friends whom I met through Bill. They each privately shared with me how affected they were to experience my love and loyalty to Bill. They claimed they had never experienced—but hoped one day they would—my devotion and affection toward Bill. This has been a stronghold for me as a long-time single person, that during my lifetime I had an opportunity to love with all of my heart. More recently, with the growth I've experienced, and the community I share today, my willingness to explore the possibility of partnership has once again been ignited in me.

## DECEMBER 2008: SANTA MONICA, CALIFORNIA:

**A FREEFALL TO** claim my life…

Twenty-four years after returning to California, working in law enforcement, raising a daughter as a single mother, the structure fell away from my life experience. My high school daughter, fighting conformity and parenting with everything she had, was the most important role of my life. Leaving the police department with a career-ending disability was the most important decision I have ever made. I also believe it was the wisest. Without a plan (no surprise) the opportunity to become a facilitator for a highly respected and recognized continuum for sergeants throughout California paved the way for my increased independence, a deepened sense of pride, and the determination to cultivate my character into one of principle and influence. It was a privilege to be selected; it fed my focus toward purpose, and afforded Morgan and me the time and opportunity to deepen our relationship. We each became healthier emotionally, spiritually, and physically—both as individuals and as a family. Growing in character led me to understand the power of influence and the importance of BEING my word.

This transition has been profound and illuminated characteristics I had not previously recognized in myself. Stepping away from the safety net of career, reputation, family, and locale catapulted me into a new, exciting arena.

*"It is not the critic who counts; not the man who points out how the strong man stumbles, or where the doer of deeds could have done them better. The credit belongs to the man who is actually in the arena, whose face is marred by dust and sweat and blood; who strives valiantly; who errs, who comes short again and again, because there is no effort without error and shortcoming; but who does actually strive to do the deeds; who knows great enthusiasms, the great devotions; who spends himself in a worthy cause; who at the best knows, in the end, the triumph of high achievement, and who at the worst, if he fails, at least fails while daring greatly, so that his place shall never be with those cold and timid souls who neither know victory nor defeat."*

~THEODORE ROOSEVELT (1858 – 1919)
26TH PRESIDENT OF THE UNITED STATES

**MY LIFE HAS** been lined with overwhelming virtues. Yet, I spent fifty years of life as a faker and a liar! "Sounds ridiculous," you say. Many would agree with you. My confidence wavered because I took to heart the teasing, all the while fervently BELIEVING it was a form of affection. I was liked, accepted, and admired—so, I believed.

Grandiose desires were met by a dose of someone else's reality, asking, "Who do you think you are?" That question became a mantra, sure to stunt any true success. It required my taking to heart the leadership lessons of growth and lifelong learning to ultimately become a bona fide original. Trusting myself and my own direction have altered my life circumstances. I now live by and share my coaching model with clients, colleagues, and friends…a model and practice that have redesigned my life.

Vulnerability and focus on speaking WHAT IS contributed heavily to a contentment and enthusiasm for WHAT IS NEXT.

What was next? A gifted life, which consists of friendships, influence, and the beauty of the great outdoors. I benefit, and my brain benefits, from the splendor of being in nature. Embracing changes revealed from the beauty availed from being outside, sharing brain science, and a willingness to accept and encourage CHANGE to design a life worth living.

WHAT IS NOW? Trust, authenticity, and truth frame my deep and heartwarming practice today. Recognizing that I have taught people how to treat me throughout the years, it will undoubtedly TAKE time for some to recognize the bona fide, well-intended me.

A shock of varied accusations and perceptions of myself surfacing in unpleasant circumstances has proven earth-shattering. This, too, is a consequence I am learning to live with, as I thrust FRAZZLED into moments otherwise FABULOUS. Not simple; yet nourishing.

---

*Weekly support from the women included in this anthology is my spinach!*

---

Vulnerability and relationship fortify the foundation to live this life of contribution, freedom, and a bit of whimsy every day.

Thank you for taking the time to read the chapters of my life! I am touched to have shared with you…in complete transparency. I don't know about you, but there are still certain parts of my life that remain deep within me, and yet can rejoice in the long-hidden, dark places of life where God moved me, despite my circumstances. As I try to gather the chapters of my life in one nice, neat little package, I am frequently reminded that our lives and our relationships are transformed by our choices. Even though we may from time to time need a time for weeping, as Joseph did in Genesis 41-42, we can be inspired, find hope, and look change full in the face, knowing that with God, we can re-write the rest of our story.

*"You never change things by fighting the existing reality. To change something, build a new model that makes the existing model obsolete."*

~ R. BUCKMINSTER FULLER (1895 – 1983)
AMERICAN ARCHITECT, SYSTEMS THEORIST,
AUTHOR, DESIGNER, INVENTOR, AND FUTURIST.

## INSPIRED FROM THE OUTDOORS IN

*I see humanity now as one vast plant, needing for its highest fulfillment only love, the natural blessings of the great outdoors, and intelligent crossing and selection.*

~ Luther Burbank (1849 – 1926)

American botanist, horticulturist and pioneer in agricultural science, and pioneer in agricultural science.

**HAVE YOU EVER** found yourself in situations where WHAT'S NEXT overwhelmed your senses?

I HAVE!

I learned how to navigate uncertainty and fear as I laced up my shoes, stepped outside, and shut out life's turbulence…to bathe in nature's noise. Escaping into nature for moments of quiet invigorated my mind, body, and spirit.

Chaos, a once familiar state of being, is now the *prompt* for me to step away. Gratefully, research led to passion and clarity…a passion to share the experience of the great outdoors, clarity of how to contribute as a neuro-transformational coach, and my ability to stimulate the whimsy that so feeds my joy.

Coaching sparked my quest to share such splendor and freedom with clients by taking them from behind their desks (or any work or obligatory environment) into nature to explore and bask in the benefits of nature and breathe deeply for even a margin of time. Coaching-hikes, in teams or with individual clients, have proven to be an escape from the fear, confusion, and obligations that can often dull our sense of fulfillment, which often follows the *unremarkable day-to-day*.

I fervently believe everyone is a leader someplace in their life, and that leadership is all about relationships. *Matters of Gray, Coaching for Change* allows me to take clients into the great outdoors for an hour, for a day, for an extended time (individually with me, or with community) to process life in a way that encourages freedom, contribution, and a bit of whimsy. Oh, and a guaranteed perk—fresh air!

AND FOR THAT…I AM GRATEFUL!

# MAKING MYSELF THE PROJECT

Pam Johnson

PAM JOHNSON ENCOURAGES PEOPLE TO GET UP, GET OUT AND GO ON AN ADVENTURE.

She seizes the opportunity to share strategies for problem-solving in both personal and professional settings. One of her FAVORITE mottos, NO MEANS GO, encourages others to see obstacles as

OPPORTUNITIES to choose a different path. She shares specific steps that have helped others maneuver challenges in their own lives. This has not always been easy; after decades of success, her personal challenges led Pam to explore resources for recovery and connection. A firm believer in twelve-step recovery programs, Pam combines faith with practicality to reach out and connect with the community in a most authentic way. With her natural perseverance, Pam encourages others to GET UP!

PAM ASKS OTHERS TO SIMPLY GET OUTSIDE!

She provides a wealth of knowledge and recommendations for these endeavors. Pam combines her love of the outdoors with a teaching background and over thirty years of environmental experience developing creative and experiential models for learning. Currently the Director of Educational Partnerships for Emerald Cove Outdoor Science (ECOS) Institute, she works to expand partnerships among public and private schools, as well as regional organizations.

Previously Pam served as Administrator for Orange County Department of Education's *Inside the Outdoors,* which are hands-on science programs, where Pam annually reached over one-hundred-fifty thousand students, teachers, parents, and community members. It is this expertise and personal experience with friends and family that she can come up with recommendations for any person interested in exploring outdoors.

NEXT, GO ON AN ADVENTURED!

Pam would be happy to journey with you, whether a personal journey of recovery or an interest in exploring a new park, trail, location, or activity. She believes our busy society has lost much of the basic knowledge to make going outdoors safe and enjoyable.

You will feel the delight of practicing gratitude, celebrating successes, and making memories when you invite Pam to share the lifestyle she loves and her simple and cost-effective strategies to explore the world in a new way.

pajohnson@pacbell.net
pamjohnson@ecosinstitute.com

# Making MYSELF the Project

*"Life's daring adventure or nothing at all."*

~ Helen Keller (1980 – 1968)

Helen Adams Keller was an American author, disability rights advocate, political activist, and lecturer.

**I ENJOY A** good challenge. During the summer of my college years, I worked at a summer camp. One of my biggest challenges was rock climbing. I encouraged campers all day to rappel off a cliff, trusting that the rope would hold steady and carry them safely to the ground. To rappel safely, a climber uses special anchors and climbing ropes, as well as the help of another person. By the end of the session, I'd lead a hike to Half Dome. It is one thing to encourage campers to take the challenge and another to take the harness and back over the cliff myself. Terrifying! I persisted with the help of the staff and campers. I still feel queasy when I remember this incident. If I can walk backward off a cliff, I can face anything.

Fast forward years later, when the department closed its program and my position after twenty-nine years as an administrator. To some, this may be a welcome change. To me, it was a time of disorientation and isolation. Instead of rappelling over a cliff with the help of others and a rope securely in place, I jumped off the cliff (figuratively) and fell to the bottom. Splat! Have you seen the *Road Runner* cartoon where Wylie E. Coyote falls off the cliff? I felt like Wylie E. Coyote. Have you ever gone along with life and suddenly felt the ground disappear beneath your feet?

All the experiences in my life trained me to solve my own problems. I am the oldest in my family and developed these skills from the earliest age. Working in an environmental education program, I had many opportunities to create exciting solutions to complex problems. I enjoyed mixing staff, students, weather, transportation, and funding together to produce a unique program. Following the closure of the science camp, I used these same problem-solving skills to create an alternative private environmental organization. This gave me the opportunity to work and use my experience and connect old and new schools to the new program.

Though grateful to be able to continue doing something that I love, I discovered I did not thrive working at home. I felt adrift from the staff, schedule, and structure that had been such a large part of my life. Have you been there…when your world suddenly changed without notice?

I tried different solutions to resolve this new challenge of working at home. None of them seemed to work for long. I didn't know how to respond, and though I tried many strategies, I turned to alcohol for comfort. This happened earlier and earlier during the day, to the detriment of my health and my family. It's difficult to admit that as a well-grounded, resourceful woman I would resort to such crazy things!

Imagine with me, a middle-aged woman during a six am walk, strategically rerouting to a local market, buying champagne, tucking my small dog under my arm. Imagine pouring my drink into a small water bottle and continuing on the walk. That was how I soon started every day. It is difficult for me to write about this; to imagine that even today! I grew up in an alcoholic family and this was the last way I wanted to behave. Fortunately for me, my husband demanded a solution. It was actually, "Get help or get out."

We had gone through many external challenges during our years of marriage. I'd had the tenacity to wade through each challenge; this time I knew it would not be so easy...I had to accept that I WAS THE PROBLEM! It was so much easier for me to face external obstacles—now I was challenged to SEE MYSELF AS A PROJECT and learn what might work. The greatest lesson in my journey, and now my ultimate goal in sharing these stories, is to eliminate the kind of isolation that comes from struggling in silence.

## HELP IS A FOUR-LETTER WORD; DON'T LET THAT STOP YOU.

*Courage is what it takes to stand up and speak.*

~Winston Churchill (1874 – 1965)
British statesman who served as Prime Minister of the United Kingdom.

**IT ALL STARTS** with speaking up. Persevering has allowed me to keep trying new options. I must admit it was later in my life that I acknowledged the need to surrender some of my independence and become honest so that others could help me. I also had to learn to listen and let life flow forward…without controlling the outcome. When I look back, I understand how the obstacles served me well. Now, I move forward with more confidence that when I am faced with challenges and feel FRAZZLED, I will learn life lessons, and be in a better place in the long run.

Did you know that women over forty have a higher risk of becoming alcoholics than any other population? In fact, alcohol affects women more quickly with more damage to the liver, heart, brain function, mood, and sleep. It can cause you to gain more weight, lose balance and react more strongly with medications than at other ages. I first heard this during a work-required training on drugs and alcohol. I offer these statistics because I may not be your typical image of an alcoholic, but alcohol consumption is increasing among women.

Today I am happily celebrating six years of sobriety. In my effort to control my drinking, I only indulged in Champagne. I know notice how purposeful-marketing targets alcohol to women. Juice boxes of wine can now be enjoyed while cleaning the house or caring for kids. With more women working from home, they feel like they deserve a drink at any hour of the day.

If you suspect you have an issue with alcohol, there is a simple twenty-question quiz to help you identify an issue with drinking. I really didn't need the survey; I already knew I needed help at that point. When I fell from grace, I fell hard. And I couldn't get up. I didn't even want to get up.

Preceding this FRAZZLED and fragmented part of my life was a highly successful career, I administered an environmental education program that served a hundred thousand students a year. After forty years of operation. Due to the unexpected termination of a large grant, I had to close the science camps I'd loved serving. I also had to terminate two hundred employees. Finally, my position was eliminated as well.

Imagine! After twenty-nine years with the organization, I felt adrift. As a problem solver, I arranged for colleagues to become new owners and operate the science camp as a private organization. I was the advisor, and increased enrollment for the program. In my previous position, I loved the challenge, the variety, and working in different locations to deliver a memorable program for kids. While I was grateful the program could continue, I now worked alone at home.

I always knew I was compulsive. I only drank champagne because I knew I could easily pick up bad habit. It was the isolation that became the tipping point.

When I couldn't figure out how manage long stretches of time, working by myself, I turned to drinking. I share this vulnerability in the hopes someone reads my story and understands how quickly you can find yourself doing things you promised yourself you'd never do.

I always loved to hike and during this time, I joined a hiking group. Before one challenging fourteen-mile hike to Mount Wilson, I drank a small bottle of champagne. Telling myself I needed to be able to get through the hike; I needed it to feel normal. Looking back, I realize just because I was in a group it didn't mean that I didn't feel alone.

Accepting that I was the problem was the first step. I had to see myself as a project and BE HONEST about what didn't work. Willingness was vital to my recovery. I had to shift from...

"Awesome! I'm in, I can help myself," to "I can't help myself. I NEED help."

But I did help myself! I relied on the skills I knew I'd developed and designed the help I knew I would need. That STRATEGICALLY designed plan began with the reality and acceptance I had to give up some of my independence and ask for help—and get help uniquely suited for me.

## When No Means Go

**I AM COMMITTED** to being successful. I did help myself, but I most assuredly didn't do it alone.

The darkest times often lead to change and are defining moments.

To understand the dynamics of ME, I had to start from the beginning. my father was difficult and said "No" to every request. This was particularly true because I am the oldest in my family and the first child to make many requests. I wanted to be different, and built a philosophy I've shared with my friends, NO MEANS GO. This phrase doesn't mean to give up; it is a chance to listen to the objection and work to achieve a solution that gets to a "yes." This also works with criticism. I learned, at an early age, to find a point of agreement with criticism and move forward with another suggestion. To do so, I developed a mental anchor in the simple formula, NO MEANS GO, which translated to me to find a reason for the criticism or objection, meet the objection, and negotiate a new solution. While this may be a strategy used in business, I innately understand how to use it to move through life when presented with obstacles.

This process is also defined in the engineering and design cycle, driven by the same steps I use at work to teach students how to design something, which ultimately solves a problem.

Define the Problem. You can't find a solution until you have a clear idea of the problem.

Collect Information. Collect sketches, take photographs, and gather data to start giving you inspiration.

Brainstorm and Analyze Ideas.

Develop Solutions.

Gather Feedback.

Improve. The redesign may be the most important part of the solution and is often discounted.

Perseverance has allowed me to keep trying new options. I must admit it wasn't until much later in my life that I acknowledged I needed to be honest with others in order to improve myself. I also had to learn to listen. When I look back at how the obstacles served me well, I can move forward with more confidence that I will learn and be in a better place in the long run.

Did you know that Thomas Edison tried a thousand times to create the lightbulb? When a reporter asked, "How did it feel to fail a thousand times?" Edison replied, "I didn't fail a thousand times. The light bulb was an invention with a thousand steps! Great success is built on failure, frustration, even catastrophe." Talk about perseverance! I admire that.

Personally, I didn't realize how at risk I was, and I suspect this may be true for many women. I am the one to take care of others in my family and work, multi-task, and work tirelessly. It was quite a shift to SEE MYSELF AS THE PROJECT. It is the rule of first aid: take care of yourself first so you are in a position to administer help to others. Or consider the announcement on planes: administer oxygen to yourself first, and then assist children or other passengers. There is such wisdom in these principles.

---

*And sometimes the simplest things are the most difficult to apply to your life.*

---

I felt the solution had to be uniquely suited to me. The most common option for recovery from alcohol dependence includes thirty days in a residential setting. I have no problem going away on trips, being in new settings. My challenge was being home and isolated. So, using the NO MEANS GO! method, I worked with a wonderful organization to start with an outpatient program first. If that wasn't sufficient support for change, I agreed to escalate to residential. This also required additional meetings five days a week, I was incredibly busy.

I love a challenge! I was also motivated to see my husband and daughter and have a normal home life. I outsourced some of my work, relied on friends to help with family duties, and received support from my husband. This solution provided a great transition plan for me to balance my recovery with the ongoing stressors of life.

I share this story with you to have you ask yourself, "What is my unique solution?" "What works for me?" I encourage you to use your intuition when you consider your needs. Consider integrating your emotions into the solution. I have been accused of keeping my life too tidy, logical, and organized. Whew! What a lesson—to accept myself, acknowledge emotion, and reach out to others in my need.

I now notice other examples of unique solutions, such as developing the vaccine for COVID, which incentivized public and private organizations to work together in record time. When schools were closed to in-person classes, I worked a partnership between a county office of education and a private outdoor science camp to provide virtual content for a field trip. There are endless unique solutions if you just have the courage to remember the redesign part of the engineering process and embrace that improvement is continual.

I also encourage you to incorporate your faith or religious beliefs into your plan. I fervently believe the faith journey influences every aspect of our life. All our choices flow together. I first saw this when I decided to call off a wedding when I was twenty-five, which by some twist of fate led to my career in outdoor education.

I look back now and realize that so many of my defining moments come from listening to the still, small voice of God guiding me. This guidance has been with me through significant moments in my life, such as changing universities in the spring of my senior year because it was a better fit for me; listening to the call to work at a summer camp; calling off my wedding a month before it was to happen; accepting a grant to expand a program to low-income kids, when it was the middle of the school year; accepting one more blind date and meeting my husband; getting help with an outpatient program when I couldn't stop drinking on my own; and creating a new science camp when one was closed so that students could still experience independence outdoors.

What resources can you consider to help you find a better you in the midst of being FRAZZLED? What tools are available to help people discover and develop emotional or inner strength? I really faith-based, twelve-step programs. I have in one twice and found it helpful each time. There are many twelve-step and recovery programs that provide participants with sponsors and service. You may consider individual coaches, therapists, churches, and small groups. If you are experiencing an emotional crisis, there are hotlines, mental hospitals, and recovery programs. Support groups or therapists are also good starting points. Many resources are available for free or at low cost.

My favorite resources are the people you know or meet. Referrals are my professional secret to success, and I have expanded this secret weapon for my personal life. It really begins quite simply, with identifying a need. The next step is to ask your friends and colleagues, "Do you know anyone who (fill in the blank)?"

---

*Asking for referrals or sharing my connections with my friends has changed my life!*

---

Asking others for referrals has led to blind dates (one of which introduced me to my husband), daycare or doctors for myself and my family, caregivers when my mom quickly declined from Mesothelioma, or recruiting staff to work at a science camp. Referrals are important way to work closely with colleagues. Consider professional and personal organizations as a resource. I find that colleagues are eager to assist if you ask the simple question, "Do you know anyone who…?" I once hired a stellar employee by talking to a teacher chaperone during a hike with students, and asked, "Do you know anyone who is graduating in December and might like to work at a science camp this spring?" He referred his sister, and she became a wonderful employee. This encouraged me to spread the word about the type of candidates I needed. It was a fast and fun way to continue the search for staff. Take time to discover how colleagues or friends can provide you with resources. Turn your questions into answers!

So, GET UP AND GET HELP! Define what your unique solution is and…MAKE YOURSELF THE PROJECT first.

## IT'S ABOUT SANITY

*It was an hour of sanity with the good guys winning, a situation where the world was right-side up.*

~ James MacArthur (1937 – 2010)

American actor with a long career in both movies and television.

**DID YOU KNOW** that gratitude transforms your life into what you have? It helps you focus on what you do have instead of what is missing. One of my transformational practices is a daily gratitude list. I've experimented with different methods, and my favorite one is to text a committed group of friends what we are grateful for each night. I have to admit that some nights I have been grateful the day is over! Most days, if you are willing to look and acknowledge, have moments and the list is easy to share. Research shows that if you express gratitude, your sleep is deeper, your view of life and optimism is stronger, and your well-being is rejuvenated. Another simple method to focus on gratitude is to write three things for which you are grateful in your calendar.

As previously mentioned, small, and simple tasks are often the most productive. I have found that the more I practice this, the more natural it becomes. When my teenage daughter called me hysterically crying late one night, having caused an accident, I had the presence of mind to make sure she was physically okay. Once that was confirmed, I immediately acknowledged my gratitude that she was safe and had the peaceful sense that everything would work out fine. I had no idea of the challenges we would later face; I do know the gratitude made my attitude one of confidence and peace.

Another shift in my attitude began while working with a coach in business, Upside Thinking, Inc. The first time she asked me the question, "What are you celebrating?" I didn't know how to answer her! I let my mind wander to all I needed to do and all that was left undone. *Celebrate?* I thought. *That is reserved for end-of-projects...quarter...or the year.* Gradually, this question transformed my journey. So, I now challenge you to ask yourself, "What am I celebrating?"

A group of friends and I have weekly calls, which hold us accountable to each other. We ask two questions:

"What are you celebrating?"

"How can we support you?"

It may take trial and error to find the right combination of people who will commit to this simple process. If you try it, I guarantee you will be satisfied and transformed by this practice.

Today, I stop and wonder how I made it through so many years without a gratitude list and the accountability group.

I also found one of my unique responses to life was to build a tradition of creating memories with experiences. This began with celebrating milestone birthdays and creating a fabulous bucket list experience. I love to travel, and I cherish the trips I've taken to New Zealand and Patagonia for such celebrations. I consider it a success that I have been able to convince family and friends to join me on these adventures, where hiking and traveling become opportunities to explore so many amazing places throughout the world!

My husband tells people, "Some women ask for jewelry for their birthdays. My wife asks to go to the ends of the earth and hike." *Haha.*

During a trip to Patagonia, my friend's daughter asked, "Whose idea was this?" I was happy to reply it was mine. This is true success for me! Our family has photo albums created each year and now some of those photos have been enlarged and framed as celebrations of these wonderful adventures. Asking the question, "What are you celebrating?" rings in my mind every time I look at those pictures.

So, GET OUT! Take the time to practice gratitude, celebrate success, and make wonderful, adventure-filled memories.

## ADVENTURING

*"The mountains are calling, and I must go."*

~ John Muir (1838-1914)

Known as "John of the Mountains" and "Father of the National Parks", Muir was an influential Scottish American naturalist, author, environmental philosopher, botanist, zoologist, glaciologist, and early advocate for the preservation of wilderness in the United States of America.

**I'VE COME TO** believe my life purpose is to connect people to the outdoors. It seems that sharing my personal journey of struggles and recovery weave into experiencing the healing power of connecting with others. . .not only in appreciation of the natural beauty around us but to connect others to themselves through nature.

I love to walk or hike and make it a daily habit. I like to say it isn't about exercise or nature's beauty, "It's about Sanity!" I have to put sanity first. As mentioned earlier, this is the principle of first aid: take care of yourself first so you can take care of others.

Did you know that going outside makes you healthier, happier, and smarter? As an educator, I am always intrigued that spending time outdoors enhances educational outcomes by improving academic performance, personal behavior, and a love of learning. Richard Louv, author of *Last Child in the Woods* brings a growing body of research that shows how direct exposure to nature is essential for what is considered basic healthy childhood development and for the physical and emotional health of children and adults. He is the founder of the Children and Nature Network, which brings together parents, educators, activists, practitioners, and leaders of the community in an international effort to return children to the natural world. Their library provides research in order to justify myriad funding, policies, and activities. Many individuals use this research so they can incorporate nature in daily life for people of all ages, particularly children.

I currently serve my passion through the Emerald Cove Outdoor Science (ECOS) Institute, an immersive outdoor science school for fifth and sixth-grade students. The mission of this program closely aligns with my life purpose *to connect people to the wonders of the great outdoors*. In addition to the benefits of simply being outdoors, the mission of an outdoor experience is to spark curiosity to learn and explore, build confidence for school and life, and deepen the connection with nature and each other. Perhaps you can explore these avenues as you consider HOW TO GO OUTSIDE.

## SPARK CURIOSITY

*We keep moving forward, opening new doors, and doing new things, because we're curious and curiosity keeps leading us down new paths.*

~ Walt Disney (1901 – 1966)

American entrepreneur, animator, writer, voice actor, and film producer.

**IN ORDER TO** spark curiosity to learn and explore, I return to my strategy of referrals. Ask the people in your circle, or the experts in your area, "What resources do you know of in my area to get outside?" I also turn to the internet as a guide. The following are some my favorite tips and resources:

Most importantly: before you go, be prepared with water, food, extra jackets, and a map of where you are going.

REI is an organization located in Seattle that has expert advice, rentals, classes, events, gear, clothing, and outdoor adventures! I recently learned how rigorous their training is for gear and every sport, including bicycling. Look at their website for buying guides on equipment and printable checklists to prepare for hiking, backpacking, and camping.

ALL TRAILS is a website and app, which allows you to search over a hundred thousand international trails. . .providing information, maps, reviews, and photos compiled by hikers, campers, and nature lovers. Be sure to download the maps before you begin a trail as Wi-Fi may be limited in natural areas. You can also record your hike, which will track your location and progress. Topographic maps are wonderful tools, and essential options if technology fails while in the field.

INSIDE THE OUTDOORS is another hands-on environmental education program, which engages students, teachers, parents, and the community to explore the natural area through field trips, Traveling Scientists, and community programs. The Nature Scene Investigators (NSI) includes Backyard Missions that are designed to connect families and students to nature. They are easy to duplicate at home.

EMERALD COVE OUTDOOR SCIENCE (ECOS) Institute's science camp has Distance Learning Opportunities such as Mini Missions or Shelter Building.

> The **Mini Missions** are a set of activities designed to get kids offline, outdoors, and into the natural world around them.
>
> The **Creation Station** activities provide a deeper exploration of the world around them.

The **Shelter Building** is adapted from the science camp lessons and can be designed at home using pillows, sheets, and age-appropriate materials.

AGENTS OF DISCOVERY is for the family that wants to combine technology with the outdoors. It is an augmented reality geo-triggered app that gets you outside, active, and engaged in the world around you.

JOHN MUIR LAWS NATURE JOURNALING helps build environmental stewardship, using science, education, and art. Keeping a journal of your observations, questions, and reflections will enrich your experiences as you develop observation, curiosity, gratitude, reverence, memory, and the skills of a naturalist. Train your mind, and the world will offer its secrets of wonder and beauty. You do not need to be an artist or a naturalist to begin!

WALKING MEETINGS. Do you know the Queen of England holds walking meetings? As a manager, I was pleased when my staff started to request weekly walking meetings. We found the conversations deeper and more efficient. I also would have five, ten, or thirty-minute routes so I could estimate the time I was willing to use for each specific meeting. Well, if it works for the Queen, you may want to try it!

WALK DURING YOUR LUNCH. This is my favorite activity for lunch. It all goes back to sanity for me and provides me with much-needed movement. I encourage you to look for local reserves, parks, or neighborhoods to walk through for this lunchtime activity. I've been pleasantly surprised to see more than one high-level executive enjoying a walking lunch break at nearby wetlands.

WALK IN THE RAIN OR SNOW. I live in Southern California and often have friends cancel a walk or hike when the weather is cold or wet. I've started asking, "Would you like to borrow a jacket?" I'd like to inspire you to venture out in the weather if only to return to a hot shower. When my daughter was young, I offered to take her and her friends to a park or natural area. I asked their families to pack a jacket and an extra change of clothes. When we were done, we would change clothes and bake for the afternoon. These memories are some of my lifetime favorites. I recall the success I felt when my daughter, at home from college for Thanksgiving, asked, "Can we go for a hike?" when it started raining. We both had learned how unique the smells are during wet weather.

HAMMOCKING near your house or during a hike. This is a great adventure my daughter introduced to our family. During our hikes she would bring along a small, portable hammock. When she joins us, we often find her relaxing next to a stream or waterfall when we catch up to her during a hike. She and her friends have used trees, piers, telephone towers and neighbors' backyards (with permission) to hang their hammock.

READING outdoors is a great option as well.

STARGAZING is a favorite family activity. Don't be dismayed if you live in the city and find viewing the night sky a challenge; there are virtual options! The University of Riverside has an ambitious astronomical club that shares monthly stargazing at no charge. You may also consider visiting a National Park or dark area for the best viewing. My husband makes it a challenge to find the first satellite when we are stargazing and creates a contest to see who can find the most.

---

*You may also be interested in learning the human history and legends that link many cultures to the stars.*

---

WILDLIFE CAMS allow families and students to see changes over time. They also observe changes in weather. Big Bear Lake in Southern

California features a bald eagle cam so interested people can observe the nesting habits of the eagles. These cams provide a window to nature regardless of your location.

WILDLIFE ARTIST, Robert Bateman, is a premier example of observing wildlife in a natural setting to learn more about the animal. Bateman is a world-famous artist who deeply wants children to experience the wonder and beauty of the natural world. He said, "I can't conceive of anything being more varied, rich, and handsome than planet earth; its crowning beauty is the natural world. I want to soak it up, to understand it...then put it together and express it in my painting." His foundation provides free educational resources that will help anyone get basic art skills while learning about nature.

GARDENING is another great way to spend time connecting with the outdoors. If you are in an urban area, consider herbs grown in a windowsill. Look in your community (or local university) for assistance with Master Gardeners. They are members of the local community who take an active interest in their lawns, trees, shrubs, flowers, and gardens. They are enthusiastic, willing to learn and help others, and able to communicate with diverse groups of people. Sometimes local nurseries or home building stores provide activities or workshops for families at no cost.

OUTDOOR SPORTS are an excellent way to connect with nature. It is often possible to rent the equipment for an hour or day to experiment with hobbies you might enjoy. You may want to consider paddleboarding, kayaking, or bike riding (perhaps a new place such as a beach boardwalk). For individuals who like to acquire skills, there are sports such as golf, kiteboarding, surfing, and windsurfing.

Consider planning a DAY OUTING with your children and their friends and incorporating a hike. My daughter and her friends had a day in Los Angeles, which incorporated a hike in Griffith Park, a tour of Hollywood on a double-decker bus, and lunch at Pink's hot dogs. One of my daughter's friends had never been on a hike before—what a treat for her! The key is to match the level of the activity with the level of the participant. A steep, ten-mile hike may be unpleasant or too challenging for some children.

## BUILD CONFIDENCE

*Nothing in life is to be feared, it is only to be understood.*
*Now is the time to understand more, so that we may fear less.*

~ Marie Curie (1867 – 1934)

Polish and naturalized-French physicist and chemist who conducted pioneering research on radioactivity.

**IN ORDER TO** build confidence for learning and life, I again encourage you to go to your community and ask for referrals. As mentioned earlier, I recommend using REI for checklists or equipment to prepare yourself as well as *All Trails* for maps if you are hiking or backpacking.

I trust you will find many new adventures in the following suggestions:

HIKING GROUPS like the Sierra Club, or local groups like the Pasadena Pacers (in the Los Angeles area). It is easy to create a group of your own if you start with another friend and invite other friends to join you. I'd recommend setting a standard time or place and rotating the leadership and location.

RANGER-LED EXPERIENCES are easy to find in National Parks, private reserves, zoos, gardens, and many regional parks. Consider capitalizing on docent-led tours or become a docent yourself. The University of California provides a naturalist training program if you'd like to become an expert.

ECO-TOURISM COMPANIES are a safe way to learn and enjoy traveling. Two of my favorites include RED, Inc., and Adventure Life. RED Travel Mexico is an adventure travel leader. They specialize in combining nature and culture, custom itineraries, private-guided and small group trips. RED leads the pack in implementing sustainable and regenerative tourism models.

ADVENTURE LIFE is a company of travelers with a passion for sharing the world with others. Their travel experience runs deep, from years volunteering in rural Africa and Central America, to research trips in Asia, studying in Europe, guiding in the Rockies, and just bouncing around every corner of the world. I learned of them from a referral and have been highly impressed with their level of expertise, smooth operations, and commitment to conservation as well as local cultures.

ROAD SCHOLAR is an organization that can provide virtual experiences, which incorporate multiple days of lectures, performances, discussions as well as live experiences. Chris Cameron, a colleague, has been one of their guest lecturers on raptors and bird migration…he will tell you that the information alone is a wonderful resource for learners of any age.

OUTDOOR CLASSROOM DAY is an international campaign to get children outdoors to play and learn at school, and as part of their everyday lives. There are many activities and lessons parents, and teachers can use with children Pre-K to college. Check your calendar and join in one of two days each year—May 20th and November 4th.

EVERY KID OUTDOORS has a pass that allows kids to take their family and friends to amazing places! With the Kids in Parks pass, fourth-grade students can explore National Parks, National Forests, and many California State Parks. Good news for families, friends, or teachers!

PORTS (Parks Online Resources for Teachers and Students) provides on-demand and scheduled virtual field trips at state parks throughout California. Its resources are available for teachers, students, and parents.

NUHOP OUTDOOR EDUCATION provides virtual experiences as well as online *at-home* education lessons and activities. I consider this program *beyond borders* as they are a team of innovative outdoor educators based in Ohio and working with organizations as far away as Nairobi.

THE BEETLES PROJECT, operated out of the Lawrence Hall of Science, infuses outdoor science programs with research-based approaches and tools to improve science teaching and learning. They work with the staff of informal and formal science settings to provide activities and strategies, which engage scientific inquiry, allowing them to explore and make explanations based on evidence.

EMERALD COVE OUTDOOR SCIENCE (ECOS) Institute provides immersive science education for fifth and sixth-grade students. It is difficult to consider the pandemic as providing us anything good; however, it inspired a virtual science camp option as well as myriad distance learning opportunities. I've discovered kids are eager to connect with each other and nature particularly if it involves hands-on experiences.

## DEEPEN CONNECTIONS

*Cherish your human connections: your relationships with friends and family.*

~ Barbara Bush (1925 – 2018)

The first lady of the United States from 1981 to 1993 as the wife of President George H. W. Bush, and the founder of the Barbara Bush Foundation for Family Literacy.

**IN ORDER TO** deepen connections with yourself and each other, perhaps you can think about who you know who might have more experience and be able to guide you. A big part of going outdoors is being comfortable and knowing how to safely experience outdoor adventures. Our close friends sent their kids camping with us at an early age so they could learn the tricks of the trade. The daughter was stuffing her sleeping bag into the stuff sack, as I had instructed her to do, and her mom insisted she roll it. I got to explain it was a stuff sack for convenience and ease. The mother had seen movies of rolling sleeping bags and thought that was important for her daughter to do. Some of the smallest ways of handling equipment can make it easier for you! That said, an adventure is an adventure because you are learning.

---

*There is no problem with hands-on learning and figuring it out as* you go.
I like to say that to FAIL is our first attempt in learning.

---

Remember when I wrote that I'd learned that HELP is a four-letter word? It is that belief that leads me to share so much information with you here. Sometimes you just don't know what you don't know and with that in mind, the part I play in this chapter is to give you that help; to GET YOU TO GO! far sooner. With that in mind, a few more resources; some of my favorite adventures you may want to consider for yourself or your family:

OLD FASHION CAMPFIRE (aka BBQ dinner) with marshmallows or s'mores. Do you know about banana boats? I consider it a healthier alternative to the s'more. Take a banana, cut a slit lengthwise (through the skin), and fill the slit with goodies such as small marshmallows, chocolate chips, berries, or ground candies. Wrap in foil and roast on a BBQ or the coals of the fire. Use a spoon to eat and it will remind you of a camping banana split!

FOIL DINNERS also work on the BBQ or campfire. You will need two layers of foil, wrapped around ground meat, potatoes, carrots, or other veggies. Add a little vegetable oil, spice, and possibly BBQ sauce. Wrap up, cook, and eat right from the foil. I cook veggies like this on the BBQ year-round!

SUNSHINE PARENTING is part of Gold Arrow Camp. Through the years, I've enjoyed discovering, and sharing, parenting tips that can help raise happy, healthy, independent, responsible kids through the power of camping experiences. The book *Happy Camper*, written by Audrey Monke, is a wonderful resource based on lessons learned at camp. The newest addition is Gold Arrow Teacher Academy (GATA), which addresses the need for sharing ideas and building community with the expertise of camp directors and colleagues in classrooms.

FOREST BATHING can reduce your stress levels and blood pressure, strengthen your immune and cardiovascular systems, boost your energy, mood, creativity, and concentration, and even help you lose weight and live longer. This can be done by leaving behind distractions, going into the forest, and pausing from time to time, to look more closely at a leaf or notice the sensation of the path beneath your feet.

VOLUNTEER OUTDOORS! My daughter had to complete one hundred hours of volunteer work during high school. This became a great opportunity to explore new organizations. I found Surfrider, local wetlands, and the Audubon Society provided us with access and education, as well as a feeling we helped our community.

SHARE AN OUTDOOR EXPERIENCE as a gift or celebration. For Administrative Assistants Day, the managers would typically take the office staff out for lunch. This became problematic with the rush hour at local restaurants as well as dietary needs for the participants. Always the problem solver, I suggested we create an experience to celebrate, which became a wonderful tradition. One or two managers gathered suggestions; we usually planned a picnic lunch and explored gardens, observatories, or a new hike; and some of the managers took care of the office phones and staff. I highly recommend this opportunity to deepen connections! The shared experience was really enjoyed, and we all felt that we had learned something new during the experience.

# GET UP—GET OUT
# GET ON WITH THE ADVENTURE

*"The purpose of life, after all, is to live it, to taste experience to the utmost, to reach out eagerly and without fear for a newer and richer experience."*

~ Eleanor Roosevelt (1884 – 1962)
American political figure, diplomat, and activist. She served as the first lady of the United States from 1933 to 1945, during her husband President Franklin D. Roosevelt's four terms in office, making her the longest serving first lady of the United States.

**CHOOSE THE STRATEGIES** that work the best for you and create the life you deserve. It's like a recipe. Use a few ingredients and add some spice to your liking.

GET UP: Make yourself the project first, ask for help, ask for referrals, use perseverance, and create your own unique solution.

GET OUT: Grow gratitude, celebrate success, and make memories. It's about sanity.

GET ON WITH THE ADVENTURE: Spark curiosity, build confidence, and deepen connections.

Perhaps now you can relate to my story of going over the cliff. My ultimate goal in sharing these stories is to eliminate the isolation that comes from struggling in silence. If you feel yourself headed over the cliff (allegorically speaking), please create a rope of support to hold you as you descend.

Start small and create a solution for yourself that contains strands of friends, colleagues, professionals, groups, and networks to provide you the strength for the challenges. No person heals without a community of support. May your adventure over the cliff be with a strong "rope" of many strands.

Above all, trust that all the challenges are working together in Divine Right Timing (a phrase I really love). I am grateful to be old enough to look back and see how my challenges have made me the person I am today. I take great relief in knowing that I only have to tackle today, and that is enough.

Please reach out if you would like a referral, resource or just to connect. My email is pamjohnson@ecosinstitute.com. I'd love to suggest a strategy or adventure for you to consider.

---

*Please! Get up, Get out, and Go on an adventure.*

---

# SPEAK YOUR TRUTH AND LET THE MIRACLES BEGIN

Susan Kerby

AWARD-WINNING SPEAKER. INTERNATIONAL BEST-SELLING AUTHOR. SOULFUL MASTER SPEAKER TRAINER.

Susan Kerby is a speaker and master speaker trainer who stands for Speaking Your Truth. Susan has helped countless clients from more than twenty different industries and across three continents to bring their hearts' virtues to their public speaking—co-creating talks that consistently have audiences saying, "I want that!"

Susan has spanned the spectrum sharing her gifts and secrets with publicly traded companies, international training organizations, and icons of public speaking. During her thirty-plus-year speaking career, she has transformed more than fifteen-thousand lives from the stage.

Susan's next book, *Help! I've Got a Talk Coming Up—Get Better on Stages,* is dedicated to sharing her ten-step talk outline, complete with hand gestures that make it quick-to-learn, easy-to-remember, and fun-to-play! Her *Ten Steps to 'I Want That!'* has audiences hanging on every word and wanting what is being offered before they even hear, "Hello."

COMMITTED TO HONOR, BELONGING AND ENCHANTED PLAY, SUSAN HAS A DIVINE GIFT TO INTUITIVELY ASK THE RIGHT QUESTIONS.

She carefully listens and hears what is in the UNSAID, to translate and simplify each soul's unique message into memorable talks. She has mastered the art of designing talks that incorporate what's been hiding below the surface with a message that wants to be shouted from the rooftops. This talent ensures that her clients get to be who they were born to be…not who they've been trained to be. At the core of Susan's work is this message:

---

*Shine your light and be found by the people whom you are meant to serve.*

---

SUSAN IS VALUED FOR SPEAKING THE HONEST TRUTH IN A WAY THAT IS COMPASSIONATE, PLAYFUL, AND EMPOWERING.

After losing her home and a lifetime of possessions in a wildfire, Susan and her husband, Russ, set out on a journey to find the gift in the tragedy. Thanks to good insurance, they now own four acres of paradise in the desert hills rising out of Phoenix in serene Carefree, Arizona. Their retreat-like home has amazing views, an infinity pool, and a separate casita for hosting Susan's boutique speaker retreats. There, on her private stage, her clients step into the truth of who they are with power and grace; discover how to connect soul to soul; and learn how to inspire an audience's desire.

SUSAN—WHO BELIEVES MIRACLES HAPPEN WHEN YOU SPEAK YOUR TRUTH—SEES THE BEGINNING AND THE END, AND COUNTS ON THE MIRACLE IN THE MIDDLE.

Her clients affirm, "the miracle always comes" and proclaim, "Susan is the answer to my prayers."

www.susankerby.com
susan@susankerby.com

# SPEAK YOUR TRUTH AND LET THE MIRACLES BEGIN

*Many people are alive, but don't touch the miracle of being alive.*

~Thich Nhat Hanh (1926 – 2022)

Vietnamese Thien Buddhist Monk

Ever find yourself trying to control the uncontrollable in life so as to appear perfect? That was me.

This charade of perfection and control left me frazzled, while I told the world, "I'm fine." Pretending it was all fine when it was not; not letting myself want or dream; and hiding my truth from myself and others, left me a little more dead inside each day.

When I speak my truth, let go of the outcome and expect miracles, life is even more fabulous than I'd imagined.

Follow along as I share my journey and you will see, the road through frazzled to fabulous isn't always easy, but it is always worth it.

## FRAZZLED—NOT MY TRUTH

*Each of us has that right, that possibility, to invent ourselves daily. If a person does not invent herself, she will be invented.*
*So, to be bodacious enough to invent ourselves is wise.*

~ Maya Angelou (1928-2014)
American Poet

FRAZZLED DESCRIBED MY life when I pretended to be who YOU WANTED ME TO BE instead of stepping into WHO I REALLY WAS. I believed that my success was directly connected to pleasing parents, friends, bosses, lovers, etc. If there were too many others in a room, I found myself tied in knots trying to make everybody happy… or as my husband, Russ, says "er," as in happi-er.

I never could make everyone happy!

The lie I told myself was "I'm happy if you're happy." Pretending to be happy was the closest I thought I could get to actually being happy. As I learned to make my way in this world, I quickly discovered that it was easier to blend in than stand out by speaking my truth.

Most of us have gotten in trouble for being our unbridled, unchecked, fully exposed, shiny, soulful selves. We've all likely heard, "You are too…" fill in the blank—too loud, quiet, rambunctious, shy, scattered, focused, or just plain too much for some people's preferences. It doesn't matter what you were told; you felt it. At least that's how it was for me. I never felt I had permission to shine. I am not sure I was ever told, "You are too shiny," but I sure learned early on that when you are true to yourself, there are consequences.

**GROOMED NOT TO KNOW MY TRUTH...**

When my older sister, Edie, was getting ready for the kindergarten school pictures, I was standing just outside the bedroom we shared. I heard my mom say, "But, Edie, I picked out this lovely gingham dress for you to wear for the school photos." Exasperated, my mom grumbled as she passed me in the hall, "She's been independent since the day she was born." To this day, Edie maintains, "The raspberry-pink dress with a pleated skirt and matching sweater I wore that day was way cuter than the frumpy dress mom had picked out." My sister spoke her truth, and my mom was not happy. I wasn't sure what independent meant, but I sensed it wasn't good. At the early age of four, it became clear it wasn't good to say or do what I WANTED.

My mom had another phrase she periodically uttered when she was disappointed in Edie, "She's just like your father." My father also spoke his truth. He liked watching sports—football, baseball, basketball, hockey. Whatever the season, when Dad was home, the TV was tuned to sports. Dad traveled around the world for his job and was gone for months at a time. When he was home, sports were his relief.

Mom, however, thought watching sports was a waste of time, which took away from the time she had with Dad to address the projects on her list.

Let's just say, whenever mom compared Edie to my dad, it felt like she didn't like either of them very much. It came to me like a warning, "When you say or do what you want, it makes Mom upset and she's not going to like you." My mom was extremely caring and generous with praise to her many adoring friends who entertained her, but she was often disappointed by those of us who lived with her.

It seemed so simple then—what my mom wanted was someone to do what she wanted and be happy about it. I was happy enough doing what she wanted, and I became Mom's best friend. Although I LIKED it, I soon realized that privilege came with consequences—it isn't good to feel special at the expense of your dad and sister.

I was around eight when Mom told me, "When I found out I was pregnant with you, I was worried. I already had a nine-month-old with a mind of her own that I didn't know how to manage, and a husband who wasn't much help. But you…you are God's gift to me!"

---

*The illusion of control.*

---

"God's gift." Wow, that was a lot to live up to! I decided my mom's happiness was riding on me and I had to make up for all her disappointments. If I lived up to that, I was safe, and it made my mom happy. Not only was this a lot of responsibility for a child, but it also had me operating under the illusion I had the ability to control my mom's happiness, and subsequently, the happiness of others.

And yet, I lived with the voice in my head taunting me *Who do you think you are, God's gift?*

I just wanted to fit in. I wanted to BE LIKE everyone else so I could BE LIKED BY everyone else. And, yet I didn't really want to be like everyone else—I liked being special, if only to my mom. I chose to hide my shiny self as best I could, just so I could belong.

For much of my life, I have lived with the unexamined consequences of decisions I made at that very young age, like pretending everything is fine ("I don't care") and deciding that it's better to not feel anything than to feel hurt. I also put aside dreaming, deciding it's easier not to even wonder what I WANTED. I figured life was safer for me if I tailored what I said to what the dominant person in the room wanted to hear.

Not that I knew it at the time, but I guess you could say, I chose FRAZZLED. The results of my decisions left me chasing the happiness of others, not my own. Instead of learning how to tune into me, I developed a unique gift of tuning into those around me. I used these intuitive gifts, the ability to stand in their shoes, and imagine what they wanted, all so I could give it to them, and they would like me.

---

*It's hard to feel love and feel loved when you've trained yourself not to feel.*

---

**WHEN WE PRETEND IN LIFE...**

**BEING LIKED. THAT** is my big goal! This mindset didn't even seem weird to me until 2009 when a mentor repeated back "Liked? That is your big goal? To be liked! They will etch on your tombstone: *survived by her friends and family who liked her*." Wow, I didn't even recognize that although I'd been happily married for over sixteen years and led live-on-stage transformational seminars for an international training corporation for more than ten years, to over fifteen thousand people...being loved for myself was not even on my radar. It's hard to feel loved for WHO you are when you are pretending.

---

*Pretending "I don't care what happens" had not kept me safe nor did it have me be liked.*

---

Some memories never die. I remember two occasions with my friend's older brothers. I was probably little more than ten years old when the boys asked me and their sister if we wanted to play cards. I felt special, her brothers rarely included us in their fun. When playing cards turned into strip poker, I went numb inside and pretended like it didn't bother me. I should have spoken up and walked out.

Fast forward about three years and I was sitting on the downstairs couch alone with the younger of my friend's brothers. I was once more feeling special—until he asked me, "Do you know where my hand is?" Even he must have thought I should have said something to make him take his hand off my breast. Pretending it wasn't happening seemed my safest choice; if I set this boundary, it might hinder my BEING LIKED. Now, when I let myself feel, it still feels icky. I wish at that young age, I cared more about myself than about being liked.

My behavior was not limited to my interaction with boys; I didn't know how to speak my truth with girls either. In high school, every day before lunch, there were girls who hung out in the bathrooms talking crap about me as if I wasn't there. "Look what she's wearing." or "What's up with that beaded choker?" I thought, *If they can act like I'm not here, I'll act like they are not there, then they will never know they got to me.* Pretending, once again, became my escape.

I took up acting. I liked the idea of being someone else…someone who always knew what to say. Plus, I got to hang out with the cool theater kids. Although, in my mind, I figured the reason I was invited to the parties was because I had the station wagon. *Pretend to fit in, maybe no one will notice I don't belong.*

Attending my twenty-year High School Reunion altered my perception of reality. My senior year, I was five-four, one hundred ten pounds, had long blond hair and blue eyes, yet I didn't attract guys who asked me out. Therefore, by my definition, I was unattractive. I showed up at the reunion five-seven, two hundred pounds, with short blond hair, and feeling barely good enough about myself to attend. I introduced myself to a man standing next to me. (With over a thousand kids in our class, there were many people I didn't know.) He interrupted, saying "I know who you are. You were one of the untouchables, no one could ever ask you out." And then walked away.

*What?* "Who was that guy?"

A woman near me replied, "I think he was one of the football players."

*Some football player knew who I was and thought I was untouchable*? I'm not sure exactly what he meant, but I chose to believe it meant I was liked, seen, noticed, and maybe even popular, but no one bothered to tell me.

---

*Trying so hard to be liked backfired. It almost cost me my husband.*

---

## TRYING TOO HARD VS. TELLING MY TRUTH...

**THROUGHOUT MY TWENTIES,** I traded sex to be liked, even if just for the night. The only boyfriend I lived with before Russ, told me, "If you could just BE YOURSELF, and stop trying so hard to BE LIKED, people would naturally LIKE YOU BETTER!" Problem was...I didn't know who MYSELF was, let alone how to BE MYSELF. Clearly, my strategy to be liked was backfiring. Trying too hard pushed people away yet my behavior seemed embedded in my DNA and felt impossible to change. Would it ever be different?

I was twenty-eight when I risked asking Russ out in early December 1988 for New Year's Eve, the holiday I always wished I had a date. He asked, "What do you want to do?" I said, "I don't know, I just looked to see who I wanted to spend New Year's Eve with and picked you." *Like there were others waiting to be asked.* He suggested dinner and dancing in San Francisco. *Yes! Exactly what I would have wished for but was afraid to ask for.*

Six weeks later, he called me to say, "I'm pretty sure YOU ARE NOT THE ONE, and I think we should stop dating."

*Wow! And I've been thinking HE WAS THE ONE.* Trying to find the magic hoop through which to jump in order to become his one, I asked, "How will you know when you've found the one?"

He said, "I'll just know when I'm with her."

At that moment, I realized I had nothing to lose. It was time for a little more risk-taking. I boldly said, "Well, I AM clear about what I want for my ONE, so why don't I tell you what I want, and if you don't want what I want, then we don't even have to worry about what YOU want."

That girl—who told him exactly what she wanted, he was interested in. The girl I'd been, who said she didn't care what movie or restaurant we went to—that girl, he was not. When I stopped trying to be WHO I thought he wanted me to be and let my truth be told, I was his ONE. Speaking up for what I wanted gave me a brief respite from trying to be liked, but I didn't take speaking up for what I wanted beyond the two of us.

The first week of August 1990 proved to be an auspicious week. After two years of apprenticeship, I was invited to lead seminars for the international training organization where Russ and I first met in 1984, and that same week, after two years of dating, Russ asked me to marry him! For the next ten years, I got to be my powerful, bold, shiny self when on my own stage, leading the seminars with my husband having my back managing production in the back of my seminars. Yet, in meetings with my manager and my peers, where there were no manuals, just me trying to prove I belonged, I defaulted back to the twisted, contorted, trying-hard-to-be-liked, fit-in-and-survive Susan. They were confused. I could feel their question, "How can she be one of few seminar leaders in the whole western region awarded the Circle of Honor for all her results, yet all we see is a woman being awkward—trying too hard to be liked?"

Not being able to reconcile my two disparate worlds became so uncomfortable for me I was ready to give up. I was SO DONE with them not thinking much of me and with my failing to figure out how to change their opinions. That year, I gave a one-year notice to honor my word, myself, and the ideal of transformation I believed in, so I could leave with my head held high.

During that last year, when I led my seminars, I was my powerful, bold, shiny self. And, in the meetings, as I no longer cared whether or not they liked me, I told the truth as I saw it and pulled no punches. That year I was more respected than ever before. My peers started calling me for help. When I was finally being my unedited self, they genuinely liked me. Unfortunately, at that time, I had yet to grasp how to be myself with people in power without having to get to the point of not giving a damn. January of 2000 found me recognizing it was time for me to move on. I needed to find MY words, MY message, and MY voice.

# THE IN BETWEEN—GETTING TO MY TRUTH

***Broken Dreams***

*As children bring their broken toys*
*With tears for us to mend.*

*I brought my broken dreams to God*
*Because He was my Friend.*

*But then instead of leaving Him*
*In peace to work alone,*

*I hung around and tried to help*
*With ways that were my own.*

*At last, I snatched them back and cried,*
*"How could You be so slow?"*

*"My child," He said,*
*"What could I do? You never did let go."*

~ Lauretta P Burns (1918 – 2002)
American Poet

**IN APRIL OF** 2000, my father-in-law offered to take the family on a Pilgrimage to Medjugorje, a town in Bosnia where the Virgin Mary first appeared to six children in 1981 and where she continues to appear. No longer having a seminar for which I was responsible, I could enjoy the vacation. I didn't believe in God. Nonetheless, I accepted the invitation.

---

*I didn't expect to find GOD in Medjugorje, just like I wouldn't expect to find Santa at the North Pole.*
*But God found me!*

---

One day, when I was stressed, my trip leader suggested, "Why don't you turn it over to God and trust?"

*You can do that?*

The next day, in a conversation with a priest, I spoke vulnerably, "The more responsibility I have, the more I don't like who I become."

His reply? "Yes, sometimes we think we are the ones who make the world go-'round, but we are not. The world does go 'round without us."

*Are you sure?*

That was the beginning of my stepping out of FRAZZLED and into the possibilities of FABULOUS. These beginning steps called for me to let go of the need to think, *I'm in control,* and gave me something I'd never felt before…peace.

The risk-taking I'd done in the past did not follow me on this particular path. I cautiously started small, then gradually turned more and more over to God. Stepping back out of the fray, getting the bigger picture, expecting there's a miracle on its way—that is where I found freedom.

Buddhist monk, Ajahn Brahm, says, "Relax, everything is out of control." I came up with my own phrases to stop spiraling downwards through FRAZZLED and start spiraling upwards into FABULOUS:

"OK God, your turn."
"Help a girl out!"
"It always turns out well for me."
"More to be revealed."

Truth be told, getting to FABULOUS hasn't been an overnight miracle. I was gaining some MASTERY at turning things that stressed me out over to God but found it far more difficult to SPEAK MY TRUTH and voice what I REALLY wanted in its place. An essential step in arriving at FABULOUS.

---

*More to be revealed.*

---

**FINDING MYSELF...**

**IN 2008, A** chain of events created an opportunity for me to put a crack in the shell I'd built around me since I was four. I set out—by myself—to FIND MYSELF in a challenging series of week-long adventure camps. There was no one there to whom I had to prove anything...well, no one but myself.

When I heard someone proclaim, "Well, I survived that challenge!" I remarked, "I didn't come here to survive, I came to leave on this mountain what wasn't working." I recall catching myself in the mirror and exclaiming, "I've never seen her before!"

In one test of will, I was proudly holding my own when the leader whispered in my ear, "Come on, everyone knows you're strong; show them you are also vulnerable." *Everyone knows I'm strong. What? Show I am also vulnerable? Really?* At that moment, I let go. After a lifetime of playing, "you can't get me," there was a crack in my armor.

---

*Speaking my truth scared me*

---

At these camps, we walked over coals, tread on broken glass, climbed tall poles, walked a tightrope, climbed rock walls, and rappelled off a cliff. Although the physical stuff both interested and challenged me, none of it scared me. In the framework of the camp, I felt safe.

I met Julie Blue a few days into the first camp. She was a singer who came to teach us how to use our voices. To save our voices, certainly, but also to claim them. I remember walking up to her, looking her in the eye, and telling her, "Of all the things we've been doing here, this *finding my voice thing* is the one that actually scares me." The experience and my comments to her felt real and therefore, risky. Somehow, I knew this was the beginning of a new me—a me who felt my fears, dreamed my dreams, and spoke my truth.

That same week, in an exercise designed to help us set boundaries—to stand in our power and literally shout, "Back off," they asked us, "What's the worst thing that anyone has ever said to you?"

I surprised myself when I answered, "You are God's gift to me."

*Really?* I listened deeper. *Why?*

I finally realized that when I heard my mom declare me HER GIFT, subconsciously, I had decided my life wasn't really mine, but hers—HER GIFT. I had felt it somehow obligated me to make her life better for her, albeit at the cost of making mine better for me.

I tried to explain what I was feeling to another man in the course. He obviously didn't get it because all he said was "You must live a charmed life if that is the worst thing anyone has ever said to you."

I understood why he said it; my life was charmed, but what he didn't know was it was also rather flat…two-dimensional. How could I explain that sometimes I felt like a cardboard cutout? It was risky speaking my truth when it was not what anyone expected to hear. But having an answer that was *my truth* was monumental for me; that was worth the risk.

On the mountain, I got a glimpse of myself and began to recognize who I was. I had a voice and a truth that mattered. At the end of the week, as we hugged each other goodbye, I heard in the silence, "Don't give any more hugs, just receive them." I had never been present to receive love because I was too busy making sure you got what looked like love from me. New friends came up to me saying, "It was nice to meet you, Susan."

My reply was, "It was! I feel like I finally got to meet myself this week." Wow! I thought, that sure sounds self-centered, but I came on this trek by myself—for myself—and am happy to finally meet myself.

On the long drive home, I spent hours listening to Julie Blue's CDs and was finally able to experience the power of her words. "All that we are, all that we're becoming, we come together as one."

*Who am I becoming?*

## SEEK YOUR TRUTH...

**ALL THAT TUNING-IN** to other people so I could please them had kept me from TUNING-IN TO ME or wondering what pleased me. With that crack in my armor opening wider each day, I was finally curious! What do I feel? What are my dreams? What is the truth that is mine alone to speak?

I learned when I stopped playing HIDE AND SEEK with my truth, I could start to play SEEK AND FIND.

## FREE TO FEEL FREELY...

**FEELINGS ARE UNDERRATED.** Good luck getting to your truth while withholding your feelings from yourself! I remember hearing remarks like:

"Don't let your feelings get in the way."
"Don't let anyone see you are hurting."
"Stuff it and move on."
"Keep a stiff upper lip."

A lifetime of pretending *I am fine, I don't care,* and *you can't get me,* kept me from feeling and helped me keep others from getting too close. No one ever really got me because I rarely showed who I was. Inside this deliberate pretense, it didn't matter how good it looked to others, inside I knew I was still pretending.

---

*On the outside, as most of the world saw me,*
*everything looked good. -*
*Until it didn't...*

---

Pretending not to feel didn't mean I *didn't* feel; it just meant I didn't want to know what I was feeling. The result? I had two emotions: FINE and F-YOU! The first, FINE, was my go-to emotion—the one emotion I allowed myself. The second was my default emotion—and seemed beyond my control. As it turned out, F-YOU was the direct result of not allowing myself any other emotions.

I was FINE.
It was FINE.
They were FINE.
Everything was FINE.

Until…I snapped. Yelled. Lashed out. Let my annoyance, which seemed to come out of nowhere, overwhelm people like a tsunami.

Thanks to the work I've done with one of my co-authors, Celeste Ducharme, I have developed a new and different appreciation for feeling. One week in her Queen Making Program, she asked a simple question, "What are you afraid of?"

At first, I thought, *Nothing. Nothing scares me.* Then, I gave myself the gift of wondering.

*What if I am afraid?*
*What if what I'm afraid of is feeling fear?*
*What if my bravado and faith were both designed to bypass having to feel what I feel?*

I finally realized my greatest fear was FEELING!

That day, I gave myself a gift I'd been waiting over fifty years to receive. I gave myself the possibility of feeling the myriad feelings that came between FINE and F-YOU. The gift of allowing myself to feel hurt, fear, disappointment, sadness, frustration, confusion, and more.

When I began testing the process of FEELING my feelings, I still got FRAZZLED and felt my default anger rise. However, I stopped, walked away, and allowed myself the vulnerability of wondering what I was feeling. I tested naming different feelings until I found one that fit that moment. Then I got curious: *What are these feelings trying to tell me? What am I not asking for? Am I not saying what I mean?*

Soon, my armor of prickliness softened, and my willingness to be vulnerable increased. I was able to share what I felt as I was feeling it. Over time, and with practice, I can now quickly release, let myself be a crying mess, feel my anxiety, tell my husband (or my friends) my fears, and trust that my vulnerability is received with compassion.

---

*I feel loved. It's amazing.*

---

Feeling my feelings has become a pressure relief valve that has allowed me to be vulnerable as I find my truth, rather than becoming increasingly caustic. My swear words were only placeholders for feelings I previously didn't take the time, or have the ability, to verbalize. Swear words never actually helped me feel what I was feeling. They only pushed people away, and, I thought at the time, *keep me safe.*

---

*Feeling Fabulous Starts by Feeling Everything*

---

## *Inspired Thoughts:* Feel Free to Feel Freely

THE NEXT TIME you feel frazzled. Stop. Wonder. What is this anger or frustration masking? Test yourself, start naming these emotions and see which one lands. Try:

Sad?
Hurt?
Embarrassed?
Guilty?
Worried?

Ask, "What is this emotion trying to communicate to me?"
Get curious, "What is so important to me that is being violated?"
When someone asks you how you are, surprise them by telling them the truth. You'll be amazed to find they do want to hear something other than "fine" or "good."

Remember:
You can be soft AND strong, vulnerable, AND safe.
Being willing to feel everything opens up the possibility of feeling fabulous. No feeling? No FABULOUS!

## Dare to Dream...

**Dare to dream** as if the world does revolve around you because yours does.

Good luck getting to your truth if you can't even answer the seemingly simple question, "What do I want?" It wasn't so easy for me to answer; I had to weigh the consequences of my wants against what others wanted. That question was so difficult for me to answer, it remained an unsolved mystery, which eluded me most of my life.

At twenty-two, I attended my first transformational seminar about powerfully living a life you love. Throughout the two-weekend event, the only thing I raised my hand to ask the leader was, "What if you don't know what you want?" I don't remember what he said, I just remember sitting down still feeling like I didn't have an answer. I loved the event and had the honor to lead the seminars five years later, yet still, I grappled with the question, "What *do* I want?"

I don't remember who said it or why, but I do recall hearing, "You know, the world doesn't revolve around you." At the time, I thought, *Well, I know this to be true! Who am I to have the world revolve around me? I am just lucky to be here.* The older I get, the more I recognize that *MY LIFE* literally *does* revolve around me (and only me). If I stop breathing...no more life. If anyone else stops breathing, the fact remains...my life keeps going.

In a meditation one day, I heard, "the only way to fail this life is to live it for someone else." Does that mean since that day I have lived my life with me at the center? Not at all! I still find it hard to put myself at the center ON PURPOSE, and WITHOUT APOLOGY—even when I know it is MY LIFE.

I have spent far too many of my sixty years not knowing how to find an answer to the question, "What do I want?" The good news for those of us who struggle with this question is that one can skip past wanting by dreaming.

Wants, I always felt, should be answerable, fulfillable, logical, and appropriate (that was one of my mom's favorite words).

Dreams are ethereal and need not be based on reality. Dreaming felt so far-fetched; rarely did I reach for the moon.

## LIFE WILL TEACH YOU HOW TO DREAM...

Life's lessons come in strange turns of the road...it took losing everything, literally, to get me to dream.

On October 9, 2017, between one and three in the early morning hours, our home, my sister's home, and my niece's home were reduced to nothing but ash following the Tubbs Wildfire in Northern California, which ultimately claimed over five thousand homes.

The night of October 8th, Russ and I were three hundred miles away. Around eleven pm, I got a warning call from a friend. There was a fire twelve miles from our house, and fifty-mile-an-hour winds coming down a canyon straight toward our homes. Around midnight, I finally convinced my sister to evacuate and then called my friend who was cat sitting for us. The hardest thing I did was to say, "Leave everything and just go."

*How could I expect her to find five feral cats at midnight with fifty-mile-an-hour winds?*

My husband thought I was overreacting. "Do you know how long it takes for a fire to go twelve miles?"

We hadn't been asleep for long, when at three that morning, Russ' sister called. She'd just heard from her daughter, "We left our house with flames all around us!" *Wow, the fire had jumped six lanes of freeway and had already gone five miles beyond our home.* As we continued to monitor the fire, we watched news cameras showing the K-mart (near our niece's house) burning, with no fire engines in sight!

It was clear we no longer had a home. In the silence, I heard a clear, concise unspoken message: "You are free to go." I retorted, "Free to go where?" to which I got no reply.

---

*A surprising feeling of freedom comes from losing everything*

---

In exchange for everything we owned, we got cash from our insurance company. Russ and I were given many opportunities to choose what we wanted to put back in our life. We were no longer tied to the various decisions we had made in the past; everything became a fresh choice.

We had to address the life lesson we'd been handed. Each day, people make choices; however, when you've lost everything, making choices becomes a REQUIREMENT.

The problem was, when you lose everything, you also lose all reference points from which to make choices. Everything was up for grabs. We could live anywhere. We could buy a sailboat and live on that. We could fly our plane to new locations and stay at Airbnbs. Friends and family reached out from all over to offer their vacation homes or homes they were selling. We could go to Tahoe or Illinois, but no, we still needed to deal with the debris that once was our life.

We accepted a friend's generous offer to stay in her house for a month while she was traveling. She still lived close. We were blessed. Not even our insurance company could find a comparable home when five-thousand families had been displaced. Two weeks after the fire, when we were finally allowed back into our property, we found two of our five feral cats had survived. A miracle and the first point of reference from which to make decisions. No longer were the boat or the plane an option. Our new mode of life had to include our two cats.

At a point when nothing made sense, all I could do was take the next right step—and trust.

> Move in with friends.
>
> Get the insurance company to buy us a motorhome so we could literally have a house on wheels for us.
>
> Begin the journey to find our new life.

My philosophy before the fires still applied after their ravaging destruction…I fervently believe, no matter what, it always turns out well for us. It always has and it always will.

I tasked my husband with figuring out where HE'D LIKE TO LIVE. I knew that would keep him busy while I sorted out the details of our new reality. Russ was born and raised in California and had always DREAMED of living elsewhere. Since I HAD LIVED ELSEWHERE, I'd been the hold-out who WANTED to stay, although I can't say I DREAMED of staying.

---

*The difference between wanting*
*and dreaming is the beyond-belief,*
*unimaginable magic ingredient of*
*daring to dream.*

---

Another lesson came from our experience—dreaming is harder when you think, and easier when you imagine! As the long days turned into months, I had several more *discussions* with God about His plans for us. My argument went something like this: "Hey, I never liked that sermon about casting aside all my belongings to follow you. In fact, when I heard it, I was glad it was a two-thousand-year-old message meant for fishermen. But seeing as YOU cast aside all my belongings on my behalf, where are we going?"

The reply was always the same. "Where do you want to go? I'll take you where you want to go."

I'd argue again, "No, I am to follow YOU. You finally got my attention; now where are we going?" And I'd complain about these arguments with my friends, who had come to know the wisdom I get from these dialogues. Still, no new response to my query.

It took months traveling to places, seeing houses we loved but didn't want to live in, seeing towns we loved with traffic we hated, seeing awesome pools boxed in by tall garden walls with neighbors looking down at you...before I got the clarity of what I *wanted*. Not by answering the questions, "What do you want?" but by answering the question, "What would perfect look like?"

We were in Phoenix when I received a text from my sister-in-law...one of my spiritual muses. "Any good houses out of the seventeen you looked at? So exciting."

To which I replied, "We saw nine yesterday and seven today, but nothing that is perfect yet."

A response that caused her to ask, "What would perfect look like?"

I remember the new feeling that washed over me, it was one of absolute freedom! *Since I don't really want to move to Arizona anyway, what does it matter if I set the bar too high? Let's shoot for the moon! Then when we don't find a house that is perfect, it won't be because I wasn't willing to move to Arizona.*

Although we were looking, I knew in my heart I was not seriously looking to buy in Arizona. The one thing I was clear about from the beginning, with God and my husband, was that I wanted to move near friends. The only people we knew in the Arizona desert were our best man and his wife, with whom we hadn't been close for over twenty-five years. But all that aside, my response this time was to let myself say what I really wanted. I gave myself permission to set the bar absurdly high. To dream. The resulting question was for me to decide what perfect would look like.

We were happy in our forty-foot luxury motorhome, so we were in no hurry. Poised to text my response to my sister-in-law, I took a deep breath and said, "OK, God, I'll play!"

I was surprised at how quickly and clearly, I was able to say what I DID WANT—after referencing in my mind all the houses I'd seen that I DID NOT WANT. Thus, I texted her at just after eleven that morning…

Mountain views. Views from a distance. No neighbors looking at our pool. Minimal neighbors in our view. Good parking for hosting events. The kitchen and great room separated. Already looks like us! Minimal remodel. Place for Mom to be in a separate living space.

A few seconds later, I added…

God's presence in each view.

I pressed send as we drove down the road to see the house that has since become our new home. Within an hour, I sent my sister-in-law the pictures of what perfect looked like.

A living room with a wall of windows looking over the infinity pool, with a backdrop of hills and mountain ranges, not many neighbors within view, a small casita with its own kitchen and amazing views—separate from the house—for hosting my seminars. A place for mom. The main kitchen was recently remodeled with the same cabinets we had just installed before our house burned. Everything! Including minimal remodel.

I've since said, "I should have pushed the limit and stated that *no remodel* was a necessary requirement." And yet, after completing our many upgrades, I was surprised to recognize something very familiar in my dream living room.

Pre-fire, I'd been asked to make a vision board. I was to look for what ATTRACTED ME. The images I pulled out were ones of modern minimalism, featuring striking art and antiques. Those pictures were nothing like the home that burned…yet reflected everything I now had.

Another lesson in letting go and trusting—as it turns out, to fulfill my requirement to MOVE NEAR FRIENDS, I didn't need to move near people I already knew. Our desert oasis has become a mecca for friends, old and new, and family to come and hang out for days at a time. The connections are much richer when no one is rushing home after dinner to feed their animals or tend to business. Sunrise coffee outside by the pool is a very special time of quiet connection. Who would have guessed that God could get me to dream, to desire, to set the bar high—by taking away everything I knew and trading it in for my vision, my dream, my what if?

---

*Now, I live the reality of my visions,*
*my dreams.*

---

Oh yes, I should also tell you, we are in the hills *rising* out of *Phoenix,* in Carefree, Arizona, with a postal address of *100 Easy Street.* I do find God funny.

## INSPIRED THOUGHTS:
## DARE TO DREAM AS IF THE WORLD DOES REVOLVE AROUND YOU BECAUSE IT DOES.

The next time you find yourself living someone else's dream, stop throw caution to the wind and let it rip! Dream.

Imagine, if you could have it all your way, what would that look like?

What do I really want?
What do I not want?

Pretend you DO know what you want; that it DOES MATTER, and you DO CARE. If you are like me, you have been perfectly trained to pretend. Let's take it out for a positive spin.

Collect images that inspire you, make you feel, evoke a longing or a delight. Make a real or digital vision board. Let your imagination run wild. Dreams need not be realities at first, just What-ifs? Maybes? Somedays?

Ask the questions we often ask rhetorically and actually look for the real answer.

Why me?
What's the point?
Who cares?
Why not? Really, why not?

What is holding you back from dreaming? You may want to write about this and then bring it back around to the what-ifs?

*If you are good at catastrophizing, you will be great at dreaming! It takes the same element: imagination. You just have to shift your focus. No dreaming—no living the dream.*

## CLAIM YOUR RIGHT TO DELIGHT...

**THERE COMES A** time when you have to stand in your power and claim your right to speak. No permission is necessary. Claiming your right to express yourself allows you to speak into existence the world of your dreams. A world of delight.

The chaos the fires initiated did bring us a fabulous home, even with all the miracles, the stress of solving the puzzle that had become our life, took a toll on my marriage. Our relationship had taken a back seat. What good is a big, wonderful house, if you are not happy in it?

"God, if you can do all this, do you think you could help me with my marriage?" I turned it over and we asked for help. During conversations with our couples' counselor, we began to imagine, to dream…of a future we each wanted, with no idea how it would or could happen.

Russ spoke first, "A marriage with benefits! Fun, play, joy, intimacy, and sex."

I followed his response with, "An inspired, playful, co-created, contributive life of joy, miracles, well-being, and awe. We experience in-common delights and unprecedented love from and for each other."

Today, I sit here amazed at how that too has come true. I had all but resigned myself to being great partners, great roommates.

Miraculously, however, I now *feel loved* and *feel love* like I never felt before.

How did all these things transpire in my life? I lived what I teach:

> **Speak your truth**—the good, the bad, the vulnerable, the upsetting, the inspiring. And be willing to listen to the good, the bad, the vulnerable, the upsetting, and the inspiring. Sometimes you have to listen to be heard.
>
> **Find your way to delight**—another fanciful noun that is rarely given the significance it deserves. Try taking it on as a verb and delight yourself. Find the delight in the little things, and more things will be naturally delightful. When I remember I am in charge of my own delight, my life delightful. Be delighted anyway.

## A CONVERSATION WITH ABRAHAM

Some years before 2008 took its hit on us, when we lost 80% of our business overnight and waded through the weight of bankruptcy, I had been in the hot seat with Ester Hicks who channels Abraham. Abraham asked me, "What is having you be so ornery?"

That wasn't exactly what I thought I had raised my hand to talk about, but I answered, tentatively, as my sister and husband were in the audience. "I don't feel like my sister and my husband are my full partners in our business making pedestals for sculpture. Russ is production and Edie is sales, but when things aren't working it falls to me in finance to keep it going one way or another."

"Yes, you think just because you took on making others happy, that now that your cart is full and breaking down, they should turn around and make you happy. But your focus on making others happy isn't serving you particularly well. And it is certainly not their job to make you happy; it is their job to make themselves happy. Feathered nests are not all they are cracked up to be. If they were to make you happy, you would never turn to Source Energy, which is there just waiting to make you happy. Plus, people will like you better when they are off the hook for making you happy."

*Wow, they will like me better when I stop trying to make them happy and instead make me happy? Really? What a win, win.*

Abraham interrupted my thoughts, "If an ornery girl goes shopping with her mother, the mother will wisely cut the shopping trip short. If a girl goes shopping and everything delights her, the mother will be inspired to find more things to delight the little girl. More delight brings more dreams and more delight. Not long from now, we see it's in your vibration, and you will be saying 'where have you been all my life, more life please,' and the more delight you allow yourself to feel, the more joy will come and one day you will find you need no one to be different to make you happy."

Abraham's, "Not long from now," was about fifteen years. I now live that life. The life of DELIGHT, the life of WHERE HAVE YOU BEEN ALL MY LIFE, and the life of MORE LIFE, PLEASE.

It's interesting how Abraham's message remains in my heart…as I live, no longer wondering about what's having me be so ornery, but daily claiming my right to delight!

Russ and I finally closed our manufacturing business after the fires. My sole business now is my speaking business, Speak and Shine Your Life, which makes my soul unbelievably happy. I love being able to use my intuitive gifts to help my clients express their souls' gifts and have their messages be well received.

I am more in love with my husband, and he…more delighted with me. And neither of us had to change. When I remember to love him first and let his love in, I feel it. I now go to him when I feel FRAZZLED, let him see my vulnerabilities, and ask for what I want. I no longer feel the need to demand what I want, fearing somehow he didn't want me to have it, because ultimately, it works for both of us when I am happy.

Another awakening was the reality that merely getting the thing we said we wanted doesn't necessarily make us happy. Feeling happy comes from *choosing to feel* happy, regardless of the circumstances. Now, I *choose* delight; that is what makes my life FABULOUS! Before, it LOOKED LIKE I had a FABULOUS life. But now my life FEELS FABULOUS.

In making choices, I get to stand my ground and take my space, dream my dreams, speak my truth, and live MY life. No permission is necessary. Simply BECAUSE we are born, simply because GOD breathed life into us and we continue to breathe, we have a right to feel, to dream, and to be delighted. AS TO WHEN you claim that right? Well, THAT is up to you!

**INSPIRED THOUGHTS:**

**CLAIM YOUR RIGHT TO FIND DELIGHT…**

When next you feel angst, disappointment, or dread, be delighted anyway.

Be delighted by the little things: the music on the radio, playing cards, someone holding a door for you.

Find moments of peace in the chaos: take time to sit, be quiet, connect with your soul.

Let your inner child know you've got them, and it is time to play.

Expect miracles and be delighted as you are looking for how your prayers are being answered.

---

*Remember: You are in charge of your being delighted.*
*Only you can feel delighted.* ***Not much delights*** *you—*
*not* ***much delight.***

---

## FABULOUS—LIVING MY TRUTH

*I am realistic—I expect miracles.*

Wayne Dyer (1940-2015)

American Self-Help/Author and Motivational Speaker

**WHEN I TAILOR** what I have to say to what others want to hear, try to control the uncontrollable, or settle for what is left over after everyone else is served, I feel lost, confused, and slightly stressed. In other words, FRAZZLED!

When I speak my truth, let go of the outcome, and expect miracles—my life is FABULOUS.

It is impossible to just embrace the FABULOUS without EVER feeling FRAZZLED. It is human nature that when FRAZZLED we seek more. Some call it *Divine Discontent*, a restless dissatisfaction with what is. It is, then, this discontentment that *drives* us to a state of seeking.

And then, there is the IN-BETWEEN, which is the ability to embrace what can be perceived as doubt and hope—and learn to trust one's soul.

---

*My best life was just waiting for me to* LET GO *of the life I had and* GO FOR *the life of my dreams.*

---

My journey has taught me that feeling FABULOUS is not attainable when the goal is fitting in. FABULOUSNESS becomes possible only when you are willing to speak your truth. We all like being special. Why hide the ways in which you are special? I have learned along the way that hiding is not the solution to anything. There is no reason to hide from the people who can see me, and no need to hide from the people who won't see me even when I'm in plain sight. Hiding did little more than leave me FRAZZLED.

One message MY truth needs to convey is that feeling, dreaming, and embracing delight are the keys to getting to YOUR truth. When you speak your truth with faith and anticipation, the MIRACLES begin.

Transitioning through FRAZZLED to FABULOUS continues to be a moment-by-moment choice. If I told you I had arrived in the permanent state of FABULOUSNESS and forever left behind the old feelings of being FRAZZLED, I would do us both a disservice. The real growth comes when we learn how, leading with great courage, we can quickly make the journey through FRAZZLED to FABULOUS.

I lived such a large part of my life not feeling loved, and all because I had trained myself not to feel anything. I lived most of my life making others' wants more important than mine. It is such a simple thing...when I remember I am in charge of my own delight, the universe delights me over and over again.

### INSPIRED THOUGHTS:
### STOP SPINNING DOWNWARDS THROUGH FRAZZLED AND START SPIRALING UPWARDS INTO FABULOUS...

Stop trying to control the uncontrollable.

Start trusting the truth that it always turns out well for you, and declare, “Ok God, your turn, I can’t wait to see how you get this to turn out.”

Stop whining "why me?" as a complaint.

Start wondering "why me?" as an inquiry.

Expect that it makes sense, even when you can’t see it at the time.

“Ok, God, I hope this is useful to someone.”

Stop trying to prove “I am strong. And you can’t get me.”

Start being real, being vulnerable, and feeling everything.

Trust that you are safe; let yourself feel love and feel loved. If you want to feel FABULOUS, you have to be willing to feel everything.

Stop thinking someone else's wants and dreams are more important than yours.

Start speaking your truth and dreaming as if the world did revolve around you because it does.

> The more specific you can be, the more the universe can deliver what you want.
>
> Leave room for even better than imagined.
>
> Stop expecting people and things to make you happy.
>
> Start claiming your responsibility for your own delight.
>
> While waiting for the miracles to come, be delighted anyway.

Remember: Pretending it's fine (when it's not); not letting ourselves dream (about the life we really want); withholding our truths (from ourselves and others) has us feeling lost, confused, and a little more stressed each day—FRAZZLED.

Speaking our truth, asking for help, letting go of the outcome, expecting miracles, and being delighted along the way have us living a life better than imagined, fable-like—FABULOUS.

Even feeling FRAZZLED, we have a choice—continue the spiral down into the muck or turn around and ride the spiral up by speaking our truth and letting the miracles begin.

Today, I consciously choose FABULOUS. The results of my new decisions have me living a life far better than I ever imagined.

## A NEW VANTAGE POINT...

Now, when I ask, "Why me?" I see perhaps I was muting my voice in order to learn how to listen and hear the unspoken voices of our souls. My past of ignoring my feelings and tuning into those of others perfectly prepared me for what is now my business. In my work with speakers, I listen to hear what is hidden and wanting to be said. It is my life purpose to see what is below the surface and bring it to light, so our thinking, speaking, and actions fully align with who we are born to be.

When we speak our truths, it opens the opportunity for more people to discover and speak their truths. Together, by speaking our truths we can change the trajectory of our world.

*People awake and present to life.*
*Ordinary people transforming the*
*world with their words. A world that*
*works for everyone. This shall be.*

~ Susan Kerby (1960 -)
American Author, Speaker, and Master
Speaker Trainer.

# CHOOSING TO CREATE RESILIENCE

Shannon King

SHANNON IS PASSIONATE ABOUT HELPING OTHERS BUILD PERSONAL RESILIENCE AND CREATE RESILIENT RELATIONSHIPS.

Founder and CEO of Matter of the Heart®, and developer of the *Resilience⁴ Training Program©*, Shannon specializes in teaching couples and individuals to be resilient in their relationships and more effective in their professional and personal lives. She supports and mediates others' journeys to design a wholesome and healthy future for a thriving life and flourishing relationship.

Shannon combines her expertise in resilience-building and wellness, with thirty years of law enforcement work, to teach others how to prepare for, manage, and work through adverse events to rise up and thrive. Learning from her own experience of recovering physically and mentally from a life-threatening traumatic event, Shannon personally recognizes the importance of resilience preparation before trauma occurs, to enable you to rise up stronger.

Shannon inspires and guides committed couples to design their ideal relationship of intimacy, connection, and fun!! In her ELEVATE Resilience in Your Relationship workshops, she creates a space of ease and learning to support couples in deepening their communication, trust, and vision. Valuing her own marriage and family relationships ABOVE all else, she shares her life with her amazing husband and their three furry kids in their beautiful mountain home in Northern California. The non-furry kids and grandkids love to visit and enjoy the outdoors on ATVs, and fishing from the banks of the Fall River Reservoir.

As a trainer and speaker, Shannon has shared her message with large and small audiences, ranging from business leaders to law enforcement professionals. She coaches one-on-one with couples and individuals alike, using her tools of Neuro-Transformational Coaching, Relationship Coaching, Emotional Freedom Techniques, HeartMath, AND Human Design. She even sometimes employs her skills as a Hypnotherapist to partner with others in creating personal well-being and resilience.

Shannon M King, CNTC, EFT | Relationship and Resilience Coach

https://matteroftheheartcoach.com

Shannon@matteroftheheartcoach.com

www.linkedin.com/in/shannon-king-mhcoach.

# Choosing Resilience

*"I am not what happened to me,*
*I am what I choose to become."*

~ Carl Gustav Jung (1875 - 1961)
Swiss psychologist and psychiatrist.

**THE LOOMING QUESTION**, "How do I protect my brain?" crept into the chaotic thoughts already ricocheting in a jumbled process inside my head. I clung to the side of the orange dually pickup, which I had managed to limp to after experiencing a terrifying, life-threatening dog mauling. I quickly squeezed my thighs together to control any bleeding; my cop brain ran my own scene. I directed the disconcerted women, who were drawn out of their homes moments earlier by my primal screams for help. "Call 911, call my husband, and I need a towel!"

> *I think I'm ok,* I thought, as another part of my brain checked to see if I was going into shock or in danger of passing out. I had no idea if the dog had torn my femoral artery, but since I hadn't passed out yet, I assumed he had missed it. So many thoughts…
>
> *Lady quit yanking on my arm! I am trying to hold my legs together.*
>
> *What the hell just happened?*
> *I need someone to help…*
> *My crotch hurts so bad!*

My thoughts continued to run rampant…

*Man, I need a good hypnotherapist!*

*Slow down your breathing...how is your heart...do you feel dizzy?*

*Oh my god, how do I protect my brain?*

The last thought suddenly expanded in my mind and became paramount. I knew I had just survived the most traumatizing experience I've ever suffered (and hopefully ever will). Even during my twenty-five years in law enforcement, I had never come this close to death. As a resilience coach, I was well aware of the long-term effects this terrifying attack could have on my mental health. I did not want to suffer long-term post-traumatic stress injury from this horrific event.

Six years earlier, following my retirement from the California Highway Patrol, I began my next life's journey; I became a resilience coach, with specialized training in trauma and neuroscience-based coaching. Only a few weeks before the attack, I had read a study describing how the brain structure does not change from the influence of the chemicals generated by trauma for about ten days. So, I knew I could proactively help my brain process this trauma.

Unfortunately, at the moment, I was still in survival mode and not yet in a safe place where I could even begin to focus on my brain health.

I had yet to look at my leg, but I knew it was bad. My suspicions were confirmed when the firefighter blanched and muttered, "Oh, shit," before he called for a gurney. I remain aware, alert, as my hypervigilant brain took in everything as the firefighters guided me around to the gurney...

the pale shocked face of a young woman...

that I couldn't feel my leg, but my pubis hurt like heck…

the wide eyes of the Fire Chief I had just lunched with at Rotary less than an hour ago.

The twenty-minute ambulance ride was the longest twenty minutes of my life, where every bump and turn caused the intense pain in my pubic area to spike to 8.9 on the Richter scale. Still having to manage my own scene, I asked my young EMT if I could have some ice. Trepidation flashed across his face, as he haltingly asked, "Do you mind putting it on yourself?" He did, however, assure me, "This time next week I can give you morphine to help with the pain because I will finally be a Paramedic."

"Really, not helping, Scotty. And if you're going to be a paramedic, you need to get over this! Body parts are body parts," I muttered as I placed the ice pack on myself.

I breathed a sigh of relief as I was wheeled into the small three-bed emergency room and saw the on-duty physician, who was a renowned country doctor in our small community. I felt like I could finally turn my care over to the best hands in the community. Being a former Vietnam medic, Dr. Dahle decided he would perform the surgical repair on my inner right thigh and lower torso right in the ER, rather than have me transferred over seventy miles to a hospital with an anesthesiologist on staff.

I could now take care of my brain to the best of my ability in what I was sure was still in an altered state. I had the best doctor I think I could have had, but you should have seen his face when I empathically told him, "Shh! Stop talking!" Doctor Dahle kept telling me repeatedly how that dog could have killed me, and the details of the damage to my leg, including my femoral artery only being missed by a quarter of an inch.

*I do not need to hear this. I was there!*

Truth be told, if the owner of Caesar, a hundred and thirty-pound American bulldog, had not quickly stabbed her dog, I would not be here today. I was extremely aware of that fact then and continue to hold the deepest gratitude for what had to have been for her an unimaginably difficult decision.

I told Dr. Dahle, "Shh! Stop talking! I don't need you to tell me how close I came to dying." In my last effort to protect my brain, I informed the incredible ER staff they could say only positive, encouraging things, especially while I was under anesthesia. Then the lights went out for me.

---

*The brain doesn't recognize the difference between real and imagined.*

---

I know that may sound weird, but this is a well-known 'ism' in hypnosis. Consider this:

*Think about a big, juicy lemon. Imagine cutting the lemon in half and imagine the wonderful fresh lemony scent as the juice flows out of the two halves. Now imagine bringing that lemon up to your mouth and sinking your teeth deep into its juicy tart flesh.*

What do you notice as you pretend that the juice fills your mouth and washes over your tongue?

You might notice the sensation as your salivary glands activate and you instinctively swallow. My mouth waters just writing this…the brain responds the same and signals the body whether something is real or imagined.

Because of this truth, it was important for me to stop negative comments, even though I knew they were being said with positive intention. I knew my brain was injured and vulnerable to further trauma by any negative or frightening comments. My amygdala, the survival center of the brain, was already at red alert and attempting to keep me safe. I needed to help my brain calm down and stop the influence of further trauma. As a hypnotherapist, I knew my subconscious mind would be paying attention even under anesthesia.

*Did anyone get the license of the truck that ran over me?*

Waking up the next morning, I felt like I had been rundown by a huge truck. A fifty-six-year-old body is not meant to fall off a four-foot-high porch and simultaneously engage in a fight for life with solid canine muscle and teeth.

*Every muscle in my body hurts!*

I was supposed to change my bandages but found I couldn't do it. As I tried to unwrap the bandage covering the sixty-some stitches in my leg I felt weak, sweaty, and nauseous. Signs, which I knew meant I was going into shock.

So, back I went…to the ER for the second time in two days, for another dose of broad-spectrum antibiotic and fluids. This was the beginning of an especially long, slow journey of physical healing.

## CHOICE AND RESPONSE

**NOVEMBER 30, 2017** was an incredibly beautiful winter mountain day. It was one of those days that makes you feel great as you breathe in the crisp, clean air. I felt amazing and full of life as I noticed brilliant white clouds contrasted by the depth of the bluest sky I'd seen in a long time. I had just attended my weekly Rotary lunch and was running a few errands after the meeting. Several of those stops were at our local sheriff's office and fire department to discover how many coffee gift cards I needed to give from Santa. After loving on the fire department's dog, I went to run my last errand, and drop off a document for a client.

Little did I know, the same firefighters I spoke with at the firehouse would be responding to help me less than fifteen minutes later. I also did not know those fifteen minutes between would change my life forever and bring some of the greatest gifts of my life.

I was taken down by Caesar that day. Inside that yard, I found myself in the dirt…fighting for my life. A fight I would not have won on my own. My survival in the yard had nothing to do with me; Caesar's owner sacrificed her dog to save my life. However, **HOW** I thrived after the attack had everything to do with me—and the **CHOICE** I made.

---

*Life brings challenges—you can count on it!*

---

I chose to work through the trauma of this incident and RISE UP stronger. I made the choice to move through FRAZZLED to FABULOUS.

Sometimes life can be incredibly hard. Life can also be beautiful, rich, and empowering. The challenging times in life need not take you down and leave you there.

---

*You can **choose** to rise up stronger.*

---

# Resilience[4] ©

*We cannot lower the mountain; therefore, we must elevate ourselves.*

Todd Skinner (1958-2006)
Motivational speaker and mountaineer.

**As humans, we** are designed to be RESILIENT. Our bodies are created to heal and renew…our souls to soar. Through our experiences and mistakes, we have the opportunity to grow and learn. Consider the resiliency of children—growing up includes all nature of experiences: happy and joyful times…disappointment and physical and mental pain. Yet most children grow into functioning, contributing adults in our world. Much like the journey of a pearl, if we did not have pressure and stress in our lives, we could not grow. It is through this pressure we can become DIAMONDS in our life.

Unfortunately, sometimes we encounter experiences, which overwhelm our basic ability to resolve any trauma or stressor we may go through. We can get stuck because we believe we have no other option, are not aware there are strategies to hasten our healing, or have not developed the UNDERSTANDING that we can, indeed, thrive through the experience.

Immediately after the attack, I had little realization I was soon to have a deeper insight into the concept of resilience…or that it would not be the typical definition of BOUNCING BACK or returning to my original shape. What became clear as I healed, was that I would return from this experience stronger and wiser and discover an even deeper MEANING for my life.

During the many months of my healing, a MODEL of resilience took shape in my mind, and I easily moved from the mainstream thought of resilience to one that is more proactive…as I put the POWER OF ACTION into resilience.

---

*Resilience-Building:*
*Prepare for, Stand Up, Work Through, and Rise up Stronger.*

---

Implementing my personal belief of resilience, which I ultimately compiled from various definitions I studied, the *Resilience⁴ Training* model was born. Using a well-defined formula where:

Personal Resilience-Building = (pr)

Resilience Preparation | Before the Event = (rp)

Resilience Restoration | After the Event = (rs)

Resilient Culture | Family or Organization = (rc)

(pr)x(rp)x(rr)x(rc)=*Resilience⁴*

Another light bulb went on when my husband and I had the opportunity to tour a local windmill farm. As I gazed up at the huge three-bladed windmill spinning approximately six hundred feet over my head, I suddenly thought, *this is the perfect metaphor for Resilience⁴!*

If you've never had the experience…the mechanics of the windmills are fascinating; they are controlled from a center several thousands of miles away. The technicians monitor the wind flow and adjust the blades to maximize the power of the wind to create more energy or stop the windmill completely, if warranted. This is undoubtedly a simplified explanation, but the metaphor works.

---

*No one gets off scot-free in this life. Everyone has experiences that can cause hurt, suffering, and pain…even trauma.*

---

But we need not stay in a discomforting place of pain and suffering. It is possible to resolve past hurts and traumatic experiences…and to LEARN and grow from them. Sometimes, we even find the GIFT of the experience. Even more exciting, we can build our RESILIENCE CAPACITY and become stronger and better prepared to manage and deal with future stress as we adopt a more RESILIENT, FABULOUS life. RESILIENCE is often thought of as something you just have or perhaps hope you have if you need it.

Like willpower, ONGOING STRESS AND TRAUMA CAN DEPLETE RESILIENCE Have you ever awakened one morning, ready to commit to a day of eating healthy and avoiding sugar, fast food, or perhaps ONE of your craving foods? In the morning, it is easy to make a protein shake, resist the candy jar at the office, and eat a healthy lunch.

Throughout the day, you make decisions. Lots of them; big decisions, little decisions. Often, each time you decide, you deplete your willpower. It gets a little more challenging—to walk by and ignore the candy jar—but keeping your goal in mind…you power through.

You return home after a full day. You still have the rest of your evening to wrap up, which might include making dinner, getting kids taken care of, pets fed, bills paid, house picked up, laundry done…and the list goes on, however it might best represent your life. Finally, everything is done, and you sit down for a few moments to relax, when out of nowhere, the piece of chocolate cake whispers your name from the kitchen.

You ignore the nudging for a while, but the more you try not to think about it, the louder the nudge calls to you. *Well, I might have just a small bite...take the edge off...okay, just another bite*! Before YOU know it, the whole piece is gone and your mind begins the ultimate query, *What happened? How did I start the day off so strong intending to eat healthy—only to cave?*

Willpower was once thought a depletable resource, so the more you used it during the day, the less reserve you had at the end of the day. Resilience on the other hand, has been considered finite. You are deemed RESILIENT or not. Current thought, however, leans more towards mindset relative to willpower and resilience. The more committed you are to your goal—and hold the belief you CAN achieve that goal—the more willpower you can draw on. It holds true, then, the mindset you maintain about your personal resilience plays a big part in the resilience YOU *exercise* during trying times. As does your commitment to build and actively restore your resilience capacity.

HeartMath® Institute shares a Venn diagram of their identified four domains of resilience: physical, mental, emotional, and spiritual. Each domain overlaps the others, creating a visual of how all are connected and influence each other. A good example is when you are physically depleted, how your mental performance may suffer, or you may be less emotionally regulated. Conversely, when your body is healthy and strong, your mental performance reflects that.

# PERSONAL RESILIENCE BUILDING (PR)

*No one can do resilience for you but you.*

~ Shannon King, CNCT (1961 – Present)

Speaker, Writer, Relationship and Resilience Coach

**REMEMBER OUR WINDMILL** metaphor? Imagine a one-bladed propeller on a hub and a blade titled PERSONAL RESILIENCE BUILDING. Granted, a one-bladed propeller would be a bit wonky and inefficient, although it would move air and generate a small amount of energy. In my mind, this blade is the MOST foundational to the *Resilience*$^4$ model.

PERSONAL RESILIENCE BUILDING is vitally important; you and you alone can take responsibility for your personal resilience and well-being. No one else can decide to increase *your* resilience capacity…or do the work. On that day in NOVEMBER, as I clung to the truck, I chose— I *will do whatever I need to do to heal from this traumatic event.*

It is important to understand the three components of PERSONAL RESILIENCE BUILDING: choice, commitment, and consistent action.

## CHOICE

**THE FIRST STEP** is to assume responsibility for your own well-being.

---

*You have a choice to be a victim or a victor.*

---

Your first step is undergirded when you choose to develop a personal MINDSET of healing and wellness. This also happens when you choose to educate yourself and take actions that will increase your RESILIENCE-capacity. You can do this at any time, but of course, it is better to start today. And you have that choice!

MINDSET IS THE FIRST STEP IN CHOICE. Changing your mindset to the choice to thrive, or move from victim to victor, actually changes the structure of your brain. Just *thinking* a new thought creates the beginning of a new neuropathway in your brain.

You may wonder, *just what is a neuropathway?* It is a connection in your brain between two or more synapses. Synapses, as you might know, are critical to many facets of our brain. Best described as tiny connections between the neurons in your brain, when working correctly, these tiny, yet significant connectors allow neurons to communicate with each other. It is this interaction, which ultimately keeps your nervous system functioning the way it should. At the end of the day, your nervous system must function properly if you expect to learn new things, retain information, and use your powers of logic and reason.

Focusing once again on the pathway, it is important to realize that the more defined the pathway, the stronger the connection and the easier it is to think in a certain way or perform certain actions with little thought needed. Remember back to when you first learned to drive a car. Every action that needs to happen to drive a car safely had to be done with focused attention, leaving no room for other distractions. After a fairly short while, you developed the skills to drive with little effort, which allowed your focus to be elsewhere. Hopefully on driving safely. (Sorry, but I was a cop!)

This takes us to the next step. The more you commit to any decision you make, the stronger and more powerful your neuropathways become.

## COMMITMENT

**CHOICE IS BEST** when combined with commitment. It is one thing to say, "I want to be healthy." It is far more important is to commit to yourself and to say, "I am going to figure out how to be healthy and do the work." As I mentioned above, it is the commitment to our goals that keeps our willpower strong enough to see an experience through, even during any challenges that may arise.

A great way to think about a neuropathway is to imagine a path in the woods.

If you start at a trailhead, the path will be reasonably obvious. The more people and animals who have walked on the path, the more distinct the way becomes. Being an adventurous, blaze-your-own-trail type of person, you are on your path through FRAZZLED to FABULOUS only when you decide not to follow someone else's path but to create one of your own.

---

*Step away from the established trail and move through the grasses, bushes, and vines.*

---

You might find a few challenges as you move your feet through the underbrush but COMMIT to forging ahead.

Like committing to follow or create a new path, part of PERSONAL RESILIENCE BUILDING is committing to yourself to think differently, to do the work, and to take care of yourself. Granted, it is easier to follow the old path; it doesn't require as much effort as cutting a new one—but following an easy route also does not help you experience a new destination.

## CONSISTENT ACTION

**WHILE CHOICE AND** COMMITMENT are the first two steps of PERSONAL RESILIENCE BUILDING, taking CONSISTENT ACTION is what empowers you. Taking CONSISTENT ACTION means recognizing what events or actions deplete your resilience and making it a priority to regularly restore your resilience capacity. This includes managing the daily stressors that wear on you and resolving past events, which threaten to take you down.

If someone followed you as you stepped onto your new path, they might notice a bent branch and some compressed ground cover for a short period, but within a relatively short while, the signs of your passage would disappear. Unless that is, you decide you like walking this new way and do it every day!

Every time you walk this new path, the more form it takes. Pretty soon, it becomes easy to see a newly forming path and even easier to walk it as the grasses and groundcover react to the constant repetition of your footfall.

Similarly, the more you think a thought or repeat a behavior, the deeper the neuropathway becomes…until it becomes a habit or automatic response.

---

*Brain geek alert! Your brain actually breaks down old unused neuropathways and uses the materials to build the new neuropathways.*

---

It's your choice—and with a little intention and practice, you can choose to be RESILIENT, engage in positive thinking, and be proactive in your own personal growth as you move through FRAZZLED to FABULOUS. It might be a little work, but it will be so worth it. I promise.

## RESILIENCE PREPARATION, BEFORE THE EVENT (RP)

*"Fortune favors the prepared mind."*
Louis Pasteur (1822-1895)
French microbiologist and chemist.

**WHEN YOU COMBINE PERSONAL** RESILIENCE BUILDING with RESILIENCE PREPARATION, you create a two-bladed propeller. Think of the power…when having these two blades is enough to defy gravity and fly. A phenomenon I am grateful for every time I get into my husband's Piper Archer.

If you have walked this planet for any length of time, you probably have experienced stress and probably some form of trauma. The more stress and trauma you experience, the more this blade is important to your resilience. Truth…in this life, there will be something, somewhere, sometime, which will happen and will challenge you. You may experience a difficult loss, an accident or illness, or some other event…either of which has the potential to take you down.

This blade combined with PERSONAL RESILIENCE BUILDING allows you to be proactive and heal past traumas or mitigate the stresses in your life in your quest to be healthier.

To best utilize the benefits of RESILIENCE PREPARATION, the blade has three components: education, embracing reality, and taking action.

## EDUCATE YOURSELF

**EDUCATING YOURSELF ABOUT** stress, trauma, self-care, and resilience is important to understand how to take care of yourself. Every day, new information is being discovered by science how modalities like meditation, mindfulness, EFT, hypnosis, yoga, exercise, and multiple others can support and help us manage stress, resolve traumatic events, and increase our physical, mental, emotional, and spiritual domains of resilience.

Learning how the brain works, and how stress and trauma affects the brain and body, equips you with knowledge so you understand what might be going on with you and inform you of the broad range of normal responses.

About a week or so after the attack, while watching television my legs began to tremor and shake. This occurred without my consciously thinking about the attack. At first this was weird and frightening. Then I realized that was my body doing what it is supposed to do and releasing the trauma. Rather than fighting or trying to subdue the tremoring, I recognized it was an important part of my healing, welcomed it, and allowed it to happen. This happened several times over the course of a couple of weeks, then stopped as quickly as it started.

In the animal kingdom, nature has given the animals being attacked an incredible gift. When its death seems imminent, and fight or flight are no longer options, the animal goes into a state called *freeze*, where the respiration of the animal slows way down, the animal goes limp and appears dead. This state has two purposes:

The first being…that the body does not feel pain.

The second reason is for survival as many predators do not eat their prey immediately but drag it off to a safe place.

If the predator leaves the prey animal for a while in this *freeze* state, an amazing thing happens. The animal will begin to shake, its muscles will tremor, and it appears to convulse. What is believed to be happening is that the body is completing the action of fighting or fleeing, thus releasing the trauma from the body. After a few moments, when this process is through, the animal will get up and flee to a safe space and will resume its normal life…grazing, mating, and whatever else they might do. The animal has also experienced an event that enhances its survival skills.

I can't claim to know the thoughts of what is going on in the animal brain, but in observing animals, they do not appear to be traumatized by their experience. Unlike animals, however, humans rarely go through the processing state after a traumatic event. When a person seems hysterical or shaking, we typically tell them to calm down. Unfortunately, when this activity is suppressed, it may create trauma that remains in the body's memory.

When I was out of the yard and standing alone in the street, I found myself screaming…and screaming. I screamed so much a part of me recognized what I was doing and admonished, *Stop screaming. You sound like an idiot!* Yet, my body continued the deep, shrieking sounds far beyond my ability to stop them. When other people were drawn to my location by my cries, the screams subsided. It wasn't until sometime later that I realized that much akin to the tremoring of animals, my uncontrollable screaming was the first step in my body releasing the trauma.

If I had not known of the body's natural response to release trauma by tremoring, it would have freaked me out when my legs started shaking on the couch that night! I could have easily convinced myself there was something wrong with me. Knowing this was a normal response, I was able to embrace what was happening and let my body do what it needed to do.

Today, when I work with clients, part of my role as a resilience coach is to use the techniques and tools designed to promote healing. There are many techniques available, which have been proven to be effective both in trauma work and stress management. Many of my clients benefit significantly when I work with them and use Emotional Freedom Technics (EFT/tapping), hypnosis, breathwork, and neuro-transformational coaching.

Let's look first at what I believe has been perfectly termed: EMOTIONAL FREEDOM TECHNIQUES (EFT). It is an integrative healing modality that uses tapping on acupressure points to help resolve a multitude of issues. It has been shown to be effective in resolving trauma and post-traumatic stress injury. When used by a qualified professional during trauma healing, EFT is a safe and gentle technique, which allows for the different aspects of a trauma event to be explored and the physical and emotional responses to be processed.

HYPNOSIS is a term with which more people are aware and is effective in helping to process experiences, beliefs, and behaviors that a person might not know; those held in the subconscious mind. You will find it in my *tool chest* to help reinforce learning that occurs during a session.

If you are not familiar with NEURO-TRANSFORMATIONAL COACHING, it is utilized as a collective of exercises and techniques to create integration between parts of the brain, which are distinct and have different characteristics but perform better when working together. The left and right hemispheres of the brain both have very different jobs but complement each other and allow you to be more effective in your thinking and performance when they work together. The brain is one of the most fascinating elements of a human being, where you find the pre-frontal cortex (higher executive-functioning part of your brain) and the amygdala (the emotion and survival part of your brain) also work better together. If this were not to be the case, or if your AMYGDALA is running the show, you will find yourself FRAZZLED for sure!

It is one thing to work with clients and resolve issues during sessions; it is another and possibly more important task to teach them how to use the tools for themselves. To be RESILIENT, it is imperative you learn techniques of self-regulation since you cannot be with a coach or licensed professional 24/7. You do not have to be a neuroscience or trauma expert to benefit from understanding basic information about the science and the expertise it takes to use it. Knowledge is always power; knowledge will make you better prepared for the next challenge that crosses your horizon.

## Evaluate and Embrace Your Reality

**Law enforcement professionals** and first responders often use the metaphor of a backpack to describe how the experience of doing their job begins to weigh them down. Every traumatic event they respond to, and even simple confrontations with unhappy citizens can be like bricks that are piled into the backpack, whittling away at their resilience. Over the course of time, the backpack becomes too HEAVY to carry any longer and problems occur.

Using this metaphor, we all carry backpacks. We all have a past. We all have current everyday stresses. And we all have worries for the future. Each of us can find ourselves **FRAZZLED!** This is simply part of being a human.

If your backpack is relatively light, FABULOUS! This means you are probably doing a good job right now taking care of yourself. On the other hand, if your backpack is heavy, FABULOUS! You have the ability to lighten your load.

Another way to think about how past experiences and stresses can affect us is to consider how these layer…one on top of the other. Let's start with daily stressors. We all have more responsibilities, stimulation, and demands than we were created to experience and handle. We cram our day full of things we want or need to accomplish.

Allow your mind to insert how this scenario might relate to you:

*Last night, you collapsed into bed several hours later than you intended. Maybe you skipped an important part of your nightly ritual because you were so exhausted, and lately washing your face or your nightly bath has become less of a ritual and skipping the ritual has become more of a habit. As you crawl between the sheets, you let your head sink into the pillow, close your eyes, and anticipate the wonderful bliss of sleep.*

*BAM! The first thought hits you like a brick as your mind inconveniently reminds you of a bill you have to pay tomorrow, or it will be late. Then the next thought slams in—you forgot to make a very important phone call and you lay there thinking of the potential consequences of the missed call. You are overcome with worry that tomorrow may be too late but recognize you can't call now.*

*The sweet blissful sleep that drew you to your pillow is now out of the question. More thoughts continue to flood your mind as you flip and flop. You may even get out of bed and attempt to work. Even if you are lucky enough to fall asleep, chances are it isn't restful; your mind continues to knead each concern. Your mind whirls as you work to make sense of things and fix what it perceives needs to be fixed. You toss and turn, waking sporadically—only to sink back into a fretful sleep.*

*Today arrived too early…you greet the day exhausted, stressed, and* FRAZZLED. *There is no time to even think about what you'll do* NEXT *because the long list of things, which rattled around in your head all night, needs to be done today. The cycle continues, stressful days layering on stress-filled nights; you are not surprised that your exhaustion compounds and resilience diminishes.*

---

*Sure, you might look like you have it all together, but inside is a whole different story.*

---

Now, let's look at other emotional experiences you've shoved down—refused to deal with—because it hurts too much, or you are NOT sure how. These experiences might be big events in your life, or simply something your brain perceived as life-threatening or dangerous. It is even possible the emotions are relevant to smaller, yet hurtful events, which ACCUMULATED during your life.

Even when you think you've shoved these memories in some dark recess in your mind, and you've chosen not to think about them…they continue to influence you daily. We have all seen the image of an iceberg, a beautiful white tip of ice sticking out of crystal-clear blue water. Below the water line is the massive part of the iceberg, the part you can't see but is big enough to sink the Titanic.

Metaphorically, all your memories, experiences, and deeply held beliefs exist below the water line—or more accurately—buried in your subconscious mind. Those that haven't been processed or healed continue to act like the proverbial iceberg below the line…capable of wreaking havoc in your life.

Obviously, the dog mauling was a catastrophic event, which had the potential for me to experience long-term traumatic stress—if I hadn't had the tools and support to process it properly. I am so grateful I had the appropriate knowledge *before* the attack occurred.

It wasn't always that way for me.

As an officer with the California Highway Patrol, I had a remarkable twenty-five-year career; I found it fulfilling, rewarding, and growth-promoting. It was also profoundly foundational to the WORK I do today. However, it also had some negative influences that held a tight grip on me.

Based on some of the incidents to which I responded, and the darker side of life I encountered, I suffered post-traumatic stress on several occasions. I feel fortunate I did not experience long-term post-traumatic stress injury. And, although I arrived at the end of my career intact mentally, my physical health was a different story.

I had ridden that old push, push, push treadmill for so long I didn't even recognize the physical influence the stress was having on my body. For the first eighteen years of my career, I worked the road as an officer responding to people injured in traffic collisions. I dealt with people who were scared and angry, OFTEN because their day wasn't going well, managing fatal accidents, and arresting others who violated the law.

Few people realize that even when law enforcement and first responders show up to help people it is not usually a positive experience. The people who need help obviously are having a bad day; otherwise, we wouldn't be there. It is a rare event that an officer is contacted by someone having a great day and graciously just wants to share it with them!

For the first fourteen years of my career, I was a single mom raising two children and trying to meet all the responsibilities that includes. It was toward the end of my career I traded the stresses and experiences of the road for administrative pressure as I was promoted to the rank of sergeant and then, lieutenant.

When I reached the age of fifty, I decided to have a complete physical. We have cardio-vascular disease in our family, and I felt it was important to just check things out. I wasn't expecting anything to come back negative because I thought I was reasonably healthy. Imagine my surprise when my doctor told me that my C-Reactive Protein, an indicator of inflammation and a predictor of cardiovascular health, was at a moderate to high risk of a heart attack or stroke! Believe me, this bit of news grabbed my attention…recalling that my father suffered a heart attack when he was forty-four and passed away at a young fifty-eight years old.

A wake-up call such as our health being at risk, makes us more willing to accept that we are all FRAZZLED in time. Fortunately, awareness allows us to evaluate what causes the stress or pain that keeps us stuck or damages our health. The introspection required may not be comfortable, but it is the first step toward the need to resolve past experiences, heal, and lighten your backpack.

Although it is well-studied how detrimental stress and trauma can be to our physical and mental wellness, there is some really good news here! Science and technology provide continual developments and insight; those about trauma and how the brain and body work now counter the old beliefs that stress is harmful and post-traumatic stress disorder is a life-long sentence.

---

*Stress does not have to be bad for you, in fact humans do not grow and thrive without stress.*

---

Dr. Kelly McGonigal posits in her book, *The Upside of Stress,* stress is not detrimental to your health, but *it is* the way you believe stress is detrimental to your health that is detrimental. Read that one more time.

We know that when we suffer a traumatic event, the brain and body will resolve the trauma on its own…most of the time. If certain parts of the memory continue to be problematic and interfere with a person's life, they may be experiencing Post-Traumatic Stress Disorder (PTSD). PTSD was once thought to carry a life sentence where one could only learn to manage the symptoms. Consider this if you will…much like a broken leg, Post-Traumatic Stress Injury (PTSI) is an *injury* and with the right help can be healed. Many in the healing community are moving from referring to PTSD to PTSI with this understanding.

## EFFORT IN ACTION

**STORIES OPEN YOUR** eyes to the possibilities; experience and wisdom provide options. However, even with the best of intentions, if you do not act on the intention, nothing happens. Engagement is where choice, commitment, and consistent action supports the effort needed for your RESILIENCE PREPARATION. This is where you create strategies to both mitigate and manage daily stressors and create new neuropathways of resilience.

Through these steps, you try to heal the past hurts and release old thoughts and emotions, which no longer serve you. Even though this requires an effort that only you can put forth, it need not be hard or painful. Recall the various modalities which science has learned, that when combined, can heal mind and body.

Let's revisit the PREVIOUS scenario and see how just a few small changes can make a world of difference for you. Remember, this is not prescriptive. Let your mind imagine what and how you can incorporate some of the actions that resonate with you.

*Noticing the comfort of your bed, your body begins to wake up. You stretch before opening your eyes, feeling rested, calm, and ready to start today. Last night, after enjoying your nightly ritual of ________ (you fill in the blank: yoga, cup of tea, bath, quite meditation, self-hypnosis and/or tapping, writing in your journal, etc.) you slipped peacefully into sleep at your desired bedtime. You slept throughout the night, your subconscious mind content with the accomplishments of the day and prepared to work on tomorrow.*

*It has been several months since you read this book and gathered knowledge that has changed your life. Your days are more relaxed. Not because you have fewer demands on your day, but because you are rested. You implement self-care regularly, and you maintain a different perception of "stress." You actively manage the stressors in your day, so you don't have to carry it into the next* DAY.

*You have also lightened your backpack by clearing old experiences. Using your favorite healing modalities, you no longer carry hurt, fear, shame, blame, guilt, or anger. You have processed the memories that kept you stuck, and you continue to work to build your resilience every day.*

## Resilience Restoration, After the Event (RR)

*Taking time to laugh, appreciate pleasant moments, and smell the roses daily affects your brain and nervous system in ways that enhance your problem-solving skills, and this, in turn, increased your resiliency.*

~ Lawrence Albert "Al" Siebert, (1934 - 2009)
American author and educator.

**THE THIRD BLADE** of the powerful resiliency propeller is RESILIENCE RESTORATION. You've read that PERSONAL RESILIENCE BUILDING is the foundational blade because you must first choose, display commitment, and take consistent action to be RESILIENT. The second blade is RESILIENCE PREPARATION, what you do to prepare yourself and build your resilience before a traumatic event occurs. This includes how you MANAGE your daily stress, work to heal, and resolve past traumas.

As with a real propeller, a third blade creates a larger surface area, more wind is moved, and ultimately, more energy is GENERATED. I want to encourage you, even if you have experienced a traumatic event whose effects continue to wreak havoc in your life, or you've never heard any of this information before—you can still take action! As you can see, the two-bladed propeller, which combines PERSONAL RESILIENCE BUILDING and RESILIENCE RESTORATION, is still powerful and effective.

RESILIENCE RESTORATION, which is utilized after an event, has three components: safety, support, and smiles.

## SAFETY – STOP THE INFLUENCE

**REMEMBER, I MENTIONED** earlier that I had read a study shortly before the mauling, regarding there being a short period of about ten days after a traumatic experience for the brain structure to begin to change?

Using that information, I protected my brain and thus stopped the potential influence of more trauma in the emergency room by telling Dr. Dahle and the ER staff to not talk about how close I had come to dying that day.

I was also careful to not allow myself to get into the brain loop of reliving the trauma over and over in my mind, especially the first couple of nights. I was very intentional to create a pattern-interrupt by engaging in a different activity, such as listening to an audiobook or guided meditation whenever I found myself starting to think about the attack. For me personally, I found when I read or watched television, I used a different part of my brain that allowed my thoughts to drift off and start reliving the incident.

I did find the week time span to be true for me. The first week following the injury, I could talk about it without triggering emotions or experiencing physical signs of stress such as racing heart, accelerating or holding my breath, shaking, or any other sign of negative response. I could talk about the mauling factually. I was careful to pay attention to how much information I shared or how much I allowed others to share with me, because I didn't want to expose my vulnerable brain to more trauma.

Right around a week, I noticed when I talked about the incident, my heart raced, and my breathing became a little more labored. This was my cue I needed to limit discussing the attack to only when I expressly worked on processing the experience. I told people who wanted to just be a Curious George, or share their own experiences, I would not talk about it at the moment—until I felt more progress in my healing.

About a month following the attack, I began to watch a television series that opened with a man's frantic call to 911; he was being attacked by his dogs. As soon as I heard the dogs in the background and the man's panic...nope! Off went that channel! You see, the brain doesn't recognize the difference between real and pretend and I certainly would not torture myself with another person's situation far too similar to my own!

To protect my brain and body from the influence of adrenaline and other stress chemicals was paramount in my healing. This included not flying in my husband's small plane for about six months. He is an extremely safe pilot, but no one loves being bounced around in the clouds. Since the bumps can be unpredictable and too much turbulence can be stressful, I felt it was better to avoid the unnecessary flooding of stress hormones into my system.

Let's discuss what occurs when a person goes through a significant traumatic event. People often want to talk about it, and what they experienced. This is part of a natural process to help the brain make sense of the event and learn from it.

---

*The brain is all about survival and it wants to keep you safe.*

---

It is normal to feel highly emotional or experience body sensations such as racing heart, shorter constricted breaths, and even insomnia or bad dreams while the brain processes the event. This is known as post-traumatic stress. Remember, the brain can't recognize the difference between imagination and real life; it is, then, important to reduce being triggered by well-meaning but uninformed statements. If you find you are being triggered, please consider working with a professional who can help you to process the event in a safe and controlled setting to minimize further trauma to you.

The duration of post-traumatic stress can typically last anywhere from two weeks to a month. Recognizing that to experience these responses is natural and normal helps to relieve the anxiety that something is "wrong" with you. If these symptoms last longer than a month or seem to interfere with your ability to function in your life, it may benefit you to engage a professional who is experienced in working with trauma. The best gift you can give to yourself as you heal is compassion, patience, and self-care.

## SUPPORT – BUILD YOUR TEAM

**THE FIRST TWO** days after being mauled were a blurry concoction of pain, disbelief, fuzzy pain-med-brain, images of the attack, and deep dreamless sleep.

Well, actually I can't say my sleep was truly dreamless. My husband said I was very restless in my sleep, which is unusual for me. I believe my brain was busy as it processed the attack but protected me by not allowing me to have memories of the dreams.

By day three, I was ready to start putting together my trauma recovery team. I knew I wanted to start right away to support my brain and body and do the healing work that would need to be done to prevent myself from developing post-traumatic stress injury from this event. I also knew that our brains and bodies naturally want to be in a healthy state—and with the right team, I could get there.

I contacted Craig Weiner, DC, one of my EFT and trauma trainer/mentors, and asked him to help me process the attack. I also added a Healing Touch practitioner to my team and put two of my fellow hypnotherapist friends on notice, in the event I might also need their services. I would use their talents much later in the healing process.

I reached out to my community of family and friends. The support, love, and care of family and friends is always important to me but was never as highlighted for me as it was during this time of recovery. It was important to do things that were normal to me.

A week following the attack, a former business coach had planned a business retreat in Arizona, which I was supposed to attend with co-authors: Pam Johnson and Susan Kerby. Obviously, I could not travel to the retreat, but with the love and support of these three ladies, I attended the retreat virtually. Trauma-influenced brains retain little information so I couldn't tell you one thing I learned during that time, but the friendship and love I received that weekend were huge to my recovery.

A few weeks after the attack, one of my former co-workers was having a retirement party. There would be a lot of friends I had worked with over my career with the California Highway Patrol. Being with them for the evening was soothing to my soul and healing to my heart.

I also overdid it! I returned to teaching a leadership course about six weeks later and discovered I had over-estimated my ability. I found the long drive to the airport and flight to southern California more than I should have taken on. A hotel bathroom is no place to change bandages and standing to teach all day took its toll. Co-author, Annmarie Gray, was in town and came by the hotel to visit. I was feeling so badly, I almost had her take me to the ER, but her care and friendship helped me rally. I did go to the ER after I returned home a few days later… presenting with a fifth infection from my injury. I learned my lesson: give oneself time to heal and not try to push things too quickly.

I must confess, as an EFT Practitioner, I regularly teach and use this modality when working with clients. However, although I have the knowledge and skills to personally use EFT and often do, I recognized this traumatic event was too big for me to work on by myself.

I was confident in Dr. Weiner as my choice to help me heal. He used EFT and a variant technique of tapping in which I am also trained, known as Matrix Reimprinting. During this time, I tapped for self-regulation if I started to feel anxious or had difficulty getting the scene out of my head. I did no tapping by myself on the event itself; I did not want to further my own trauma by not holding the safe space necessary to process and resolve trauma alone.

I welcomed the awareness of another complementary energy healing modality: Healing Touch, which is used by many nurses in hospitals to help patients in their healing process, as well as by other energy healers. I experienced considerable healing and forgiveness work during these sessions.

During the first couple of weeks after the attack, returning to normal felt important...possibly the desire to feel ordinary. The little things—when I went to my friend's retirement party or returned to teaching—made me feel better. However, they also exhausted me! Another lesson: the importance to honor the need for my body to rest so it could heal—and balance what my mind needed to feel safe and heal.

My essential needs changed daily; they are different for everyone. It is important to listen to what you need when your goal is to heal. There is no right or wrong...only what is right for you.

## SMILE – RECOGNIZE THE GIFTS

**WORKING WITH DR.** Craig Weiner, I had processed most aspects of the attack within the first few sessions, using EFT and Matrix

Reimprinting, a special form of tapping developed by Karl Dawson. In this special method, the focus is to transform painful memories that keep people stuck in the past. By the third or fourth session, I was beginning to realize the GIFTS of this traumatic event. There were several that I learned of relatively soon.

The first was the love and support of my family and friends who rallied around me. I am predominately an independent woman whose purpose is to support others. Thus, it was relatively new to me to realize the physical and emotional care I needed. The physical healing was very difficult; my husband had to help with some of the initial care to adhere the steri-strips needed to hold the wound closed after the stitches were removed.

The extreme challenge was to take care of my leg. Because dog bites are so dirty, and my leg wound was so deep, it had to heal from the inside out. I experienced five infections over the two months it took to close. This meant five rounds of broad-spectrum antibiotics, which did a number on my body.

My new daily routine? To dress my wounds twice a day with wet-to-dry dressings to draw out infection. Did I say daily? I had to follow the practice for almost two months. Each time I looked at my injuries I was saddened to see the damage to my body. I was forced every day to look at my new normal. Worse, I had to smell it! I don't mean to be gross, but I am compelled to share because these experiences are all aspects, of which you must be aware, which can lead to a traumatic experience, grasp your very being, and impose upon you a long-term trauma. I am grateful to have had Dr. Weiner to work with on this issue.

Finally, my leg wound healed enough I could stop the wet-to-dry bandages and apply weekly derma skin adhesive ones. Granted, it was great to not have to change the dressings several times a day, but can I say pulling off those darn adhesives every week was just another insult to injury. Dang, those hurt!

After a couple more months of wearing the derma skin, I was referred to a plastic surgeon. A wonderful man who ordered me to massage the facia around my scar daily, "and make it hurt," he said as he squeezed into my scar area. Anyone who knows what it feels like to massage scar tissue knows this is a daily dose of *no fun*.

About six months after the attack, I realized I was not walking normally, but in such a way I protected my leg. I expressed my frustration to my husband that the tendons behind my knee hurt, which didn't seem right…they were about four inches away from the actual injury. "Honey, your muscle had to be sewn back together, it's shorter," he stated in his patient, yet factual manner. At that moment I realized I had to be intentional if I were to walk normally again.

As I healed and challenged my struggles, I recognized how incredible my body is—that it could survive so much damage and still heal. Every time I looked at my injury and saw the beauty of strength represented in my scar, I grew further from being traumatized. The healing is not only a testament to how extraordinarily we are created but how RESILIENT we are meant to be.

During this time, I also realized many of my previous experiences and what I learned from them, had prepared me to *thrive* as I healed. All the resilience and trauma training I had completed helped me recognize the ways it can affect you and the modalities available to help resolve the anguish.

An even more amazing gift was given in the opportunity to live through and examine this extremely intense trauma from the perspective of a resilience coach and the work I do with my clients. In addition, the system of *Resilience*[4] Training Program© was created.

To be honest, I am beyond grateful for the gift to help others UNDERSTAND they can indeed heal from the traumatic experiences in their lives. I have clearly told the Lord I would prefer to not have to experience anything like that again; Message received!

Finally, the greatest gift for me was my own spiritual growth. I embrace the gift of life every day. I am so grateful not only for my life but that I can be here for my husband and children, and to watch my grandkids grow.

The focus on the gifts I received from what was a horrific experience obliges me to address a lesser-known concept in the realm of trauma—the theory of Post-Traumatic Growth (PTG), developed by psychologists Richard Tedeschi, Ph.D., and Lawrence Calhoun, Ph.D. They identify five areas that people who have gone through trauma and experienced post-traumatic stress injury might grow in:

New Possibilities
Appreciation of Life
Relating to Others
Personal Strength
Spiritual Changes

The theory posits that PTG is not a guarantee when one experiences trauma and major struggles should not be looked at as something to seek, but PTG is common. What I found when working with clients or teaching students is that gifts can come out of challenges and perspectives of individual experiences… changes their perspective on their own healing.

Peter A. Levin, Ph.D., author and the founder of Somatic Experiencing,™ writes in *Waking the Tiger*, "…trauma is a fact of life. It does not, however, have to be a life sentence. Not only can trauma be healed but with proper guidance and support, it can be transformative."

---

*Trauma does not have to be a life sentence, and neither does healing from it. The experience can be transformative.*

---

An important part of thriving through trauma is belief and attitude. An understanding of traumatic experiences is it is not the experience itself that traumatizes a person, but their attitude and response to it.

You might not recognize the gift for a while, or you might recognize it right away. There is no right or wrong here; what is important is to recognize you are a survivor and have the opportunity to thrive…to rise up stronger.

## RESILIENT CULTURE, ORGANIZATION OR FAMILY (RC)

*"In order to succeed, people need a sense of self-efficacy, to struggle together with resilience to meet the inevitable obstacles and inequities of life."*

~ Albert Bandura (1925 - 2021)
Canadian-born American psychologist and originator of social cognitive theory.

**WITH THE FIRST** three blades of resilience, PERSONAL RESILIENCE BUILDING, RESILIENCE PREPARATION, AND RESILIENCE RESTORATION, you now have a strong foundation for building your resilience capacity. The fourth blade, RESILIENT CULTURE, ORGANIZATION OR FAMILY strengthens the outcome of successful resilience capacity building.

When I first developed the *Resilience⁴ Training Program,* it was in the context of working with law enforcement and first responders. Thus, my focus was on organizations or agencies. As I healed from my own trauma and worked with my clients in their healing, I came to recognize the importance of the family as a culture as well.

Immediately following my traumatic experience with Caesar, friends and family reached out to me. With social media, word spread quickly and many of my former co-workers from the California Highway Patrol reached out to offer support. Each brought me understanding, comfort, and/or support.

Matthew Lindholm, a former academy training officer and a respected friend, helped assuage my belief I may have been responsible for the attack. I struggled with the *why* and questioned whether I had done something to cause the attack. Matthew has vast experience with pit bulls and American bulldogs and offered me insight into the breed. When the owner of Caesar opened the door, two small dachshunds ran out and barked at my feet. As I stood there letting them smell me, one bit me on the ankle. Then Caesar attacked. Everything happened within seconds. Matthew explained it was most likely the actions of the two dachshunds that instigated the attack because of the highly driven pack mentality of the American bulldog breed.

With this knowledge, I was greatly relieved; it helped me understand it was nothing personal; it was nothing deserved. Caesar had simply responded to a dog's natural instinct. Once I understood the dynamics, it played a huge part in my healing and forgiveness.

## The Look of a Resilient Culture

**A resilient culture** can look like different groups of people. It can be an organization, a family unit, a couple. The four other women with whom I am writing this book are part of my RESILIENT CULTURE. For over five years we've been friends, accountability partners, and mentors for one another. We set an intention to hold a weekly morning call; we consistently check in, share, and support each other. It is never a complaint fest! We do not impose upon others to wallow in our MISERIES; we speak encouragement, positivity, and truthfulness to each other, even when it may initially hurt. Many times, we pray for each other, but most importantly, we know we are there FOR each other. We are committed to the following components, which apply for building a RESILIENT CULTURE: loyalty to the health and well-being of all members, creating a language of resilience, and using laughter and gratitude to raise the spirit.

## Loyalty to the Health and Well-being of all Members

**Much in alignment** with the choice, commitment, and consistent action of PERSONAL RESPONSIBILITY, the loyalty needed to create a RESILIENT CULTURE always begins with a choice, commitment, and consistent action. There must be a commitment by each member to make the health and well-being of all members a high priority.

Life happens. That is a given. Being proactive comes into play when a culture equips itself with tools and creates an environment that supports the resilience of its members. Today is a great time to start!

Just as the powerful blades of RESILIENCE PREPARATION and RESILIENCE RESTORATION are essential for the individual, they are also imperative for the culture and community. As family members, we all carry past hurts, stresses, and bricks that add weight to our backpacks. It is a given, we will all experience loss, challenges, and personal stress in the future. Fortunately, the more effort we put into action as we resolve, heal, and prepare for these inevitable life experiences, the better we can thrive and rise up stronger as a family.

Loyalty can mean different things to different people. For the sake of this topic, let's look at what loyalty to creating a RESILIENT CULTURE might include:

Commitment to *putting the relationship and family first*. It is easier and more effective to ensure the readiness and waterproofing of your boat before you launch than it is to bail water out of your boat while it is sinking. Most people would say they are committed to their relationships, and they probably are, but have they taken the actions to make the relationship RESILIENT?

Dedication to *being responsible for your own well-being and personal growth.* PERSONAL RESILIENCE BUILDING shows us that others can't build our resilience for us; we must do that ourselves. If we haven't done our own work, it will be more challenging to support others in our community who are hurting...and not get pulled into their trauma-drama ourselves.

Two primary dangers for a first-line worker who comes to the aid of people who hurt physically or mentally include compassion fatigue or vicarious trauma. Both can occur when the first-line worker fails to take care of themselves first. If they haven't done their own healing work and continue with self-care regularly, they may very well find themselves depleted and/or personally being traumatized by the other person's trauma.

As you have read in my story, taking responsibility and implementing the steps used in RESILIENCE PREPARATION will support you in being more effective as a part of your RESILIENT CULTURE.

Commitment to recognizing *it is not our job to fix another person*, but rather to see that person as whole and capable. Truth is, you fix no one. That can be a hard realization, especially when someone you love is hurting. In coaching, we work from a place that everyone has the capacity and personal wisdom to know what they need to grow and heal.

The role of a coach is not to tell a person what they need, but to coach, ask questions, and support them as they discover within themselves those answers. Even when using modalities: EFT, neuro-transformational coaching, or hypnosis, the behavior modification is done within the coaching model and is client-led.

Within your family or community, you can support a person by being curious and asking questions, and holding that person in love, rather than to give advice. Answers are much more valuable when they come from within rather than being told what to do.

Promise to always *respond from a place of love.* I know as humans we cannot always make this mark, but when we set the intention, we will do it more often than if we don't make a commitment. So, what do I mean? Do I think you don't respond with love to your loved one? Of course not! But, when stress is high or the pain of trauma is being felt, emotions typically run high...resulting in shorter tempers or inadvertent hurtful behavior. Having the intention to always respond in love and assuming positive intention by the other person can help you to make a choice that is more supportive of the community. Responding to yourself from a place of love is equally important.

Commitment to *create a solid environment of open communication.* Open communication creates a space of safety that allows for truth, vulnerability, and acceptance. After a traumatic incident or during a time of high stress, it is important for a person to have a safe place to share the emotions, thoughts, fears, insights, a-ha's, etc. with others who will hold that space for them. Open communication is a practice that is more effective if it is developed before something of major import happens. Trying to create safe communication when you already have the added stress of someone who is struggling is possible, but it may be more of a challenge to create that safe container.

## Language of Resilience

**Sticks and stones** *may break my bones, but words will never hurt me.* Do you remember singing that little rhyme as a kid when another kid taunted you? We all know that people we care about can sometimes say things that hurt our feelings…rub us the wrong way, even when what they said may have come from a vastly different perspective or said unintentionally.

Interestingly, however, often worse than what others say to us is what we say to ourselves. You may have read that according to the National Science Foundation, on average people have between twelve thousand to sixty thousand thoughts per day. What may also astonish you is that eighty percent of those thoughts are negative, and ninety-five percent are repetitive. That's a lot of repeating negative thoughts!

Remember the neuropathway you read about earlier? The more we think a negative thought over and over again, the deeper and more defined that neuropathway becomes. In fact, these pathways become so defined we may no longer recognize them when we talk badly to ourselves. Some of us say things to ourselves that we would never speak to another person! To build a RESILIENT MINDSET is to become aware of the non-productive, negative thoughts and build new, more affirming, and supportive pathways.

Conversely, listen to the stories in your culture. What are the repetitive stories that are told in your family that are not supportive or uplifting of all your family members? Many of these are passed down through generations. Start paying attention and listen to determine whether ideas and comments are negative or positive for your resilience. Our words DO matter.

So, what does RESILIENT LANGUAGE look like? Maybe we should start with what it doesn't look like.

You will remember that I had to protect my brain from further trauma in the emergency room when Dr. Dahle kept telling me how close I was to almost being killed by the dog. I know he was well-meaning. In fact, many of the things people tried to say to me were well-meaning but most assuredly not supportive of my healing.

I heard various forms of, "Oh my gosh! You're going to have PTSD for the rest of your life!" or "You will never get over this!" or "You will be afraid of dogs forever!" None of which were true or supportive in my healing.

Knowing how detrimental hearing others' traumatic stories could be, I was attentive to when people wanted to share their own stories of dog encounters. Much like not wanting to listen to the television show where the man was being attacked by his own dogs, I did not need to hear the stories of others' traumatic experiences…until I had healed my own.

In all cases, I believe people were well-intended and wanted to be supportive. They didn't know how it affected me, and it remained my responsibility to protect my own brain. It is just as important to be intentional and not use language that can cause further trauma within your family.

RESILIENT LANGUAGE is supportive, encouraging, and truth based. In the RESILIENCE PREPARATION mode, it is vital to check your stories and comments, and take action to rid your vocabulary of those that don't support you or your family. In the words of my friend, Celeste, "get rid of the stinking thinking!" Start to speak the language of gratitude and encouragement within your community and you will ultimately change your neuropathways for the good.

In the RESILIENCE RESTORATION mode, after a traumatic experience or during a highly stressful time, the above language would also apply; CHECKING for comments that don't support or empower each other. It is far better to speak from a place of healing and resolve the trauma. The important things I needed to hear were, "I'm here," "How can I help?" "I know this is really HARD and it's ok to feel that." "You got this!"

## LAUGHTER AND GRATITUDE TO RAISE THE SPIRIT

**"LAUGHTER IS THE** best medicine" is an age-old adage attributed to Henri de Mondeville, a professor of surgery in the 1300's. Many of us grew up hearing this phrase and science now supports it is, indeed, true.

Laughter does so much for your health and well-being, including elevating your mood and boosting your immune system. When we laugh, we flood our system with many wonderful chemicals that counter the chemicals of stress. A good laugh produces a rush of feel-good endorphins…nature's pain reliever. Laughing helps shift our mental state, increase our pain threshold, and improve our healing. It can also bond us with others and increase our bonding hormone, oxytocin.

Even as I clung to the side of the truck after the attack, I was able to see the irony of having to coordinate my own help. I surprised myself when I humorously said, "Oh my God, I need a good hypnotherapist," and Caesar's owner leaned over and replied, "You are one!"

Relating the story of the sweet and rather timid EMT always makes me laugh and usually provides a ripple of giggles throughout my audience.

This is not to diminish the seriousness of any trauma or the stressful situations you experience. But, when we focus on the dark and gloomy, we keep our brain trapped within the trauma. When we focus on the negative, all we can see is negative.

---

*If we keep telling our victim stories, we fail to see our victor selves.*

---

Laughter also helps us learn. When we laugh and the brain is washed in our feel-good chemicals, it feels safe and we shift to using the pre-frontal cortex and higher thinking functions, which allows our brains to learn.

My lively grandson, Jackson, used to tell us, "Find your attitude of gratitude!"

Ah! The wisdom of young minds.

Somehow, Jackson had figured out early on that it is impossible to have a grateful mindset and stay in negative thinking. Unfortunately, our brains are wired to seek and respond to negative thinking and will dismiss a positive experience in search of potential danger. It is a survival skill that kept our ancestors alive. And…stopping to smell the roses could have set up a caveman to be the sabretooth tiger's dinner!

Even though we live in a much safer world today, our brain still operates the same way. It is estimated we require ten positive experiences to counter a negative, but if we're not paying attention, we don't even recognize the positive!

When you choose to create a practice to be grateful and mindful of your blessings, you will be supported as you shift to a more RESILIENT MINDSET. In your efforts to develop your

RESILIENT CULTURE, be proactive. Stop and create opportunities to laugh together and share your gratitude.

I trust you have enjoyed my story; that you gleaned hope for the RESILIENCE that is possible in your life as well. As a recap, *Resilience[4]* is the name of my program, and the four steps that get you there include:

1. Personal Resilience Building
2. Resilience Preparation
3. Resilience Restoration
4. Resilience Culture

As we all learn to cope in these uncertain times with love and compassion, it is essential we have hope in the RESILIENCE within—to rise above these troubling times with courage and creativity. Together, we will rise through these trying times, stronger, kinder, and more resilient.

---

*Rise Up Stronger.*
*What takes me down, does not have to take me out.*
*Every day I rise up stronger.*

---

Viktor E. Frankl, an Austrian psychotherapist, and neurologist was a Holocaust survivor who lost his entire family in the concentration camps. His book, *Man's Search for Meaning* describes the indescribable horrors of his four years spent as a prisoner in four different camps. More importantly, he shares his survival and what kept him motivated to live every day.

When he was released from his imprisonment, he returned to his practice of psychology and helped others to discover their meaning in life and reclaim their mental wellness. One cannot read his writing without being touched by his insights and multiple nuggets of wisdom about the resilience of humankind. We are created to be RESILIENT even THROUGH the most horrendous experiences life can BRING.

While I have several favorite quotes from Frankl's Man's Search for Meaning, the one I resonate with the most is, "Between stimulus and response there is a space. In that space is our power to choose our response. In our response lies our growth and our freedom."

We don't always get to choose the stimulus life brings us. But we always have the CHOICE TO CHOOSE our response. With commitment and work, we have a choice.

We have the choice to **choose to** be a victor.
We have the choice to move through FRAZZLED to FABULOUS.
We have the choice to RISE UP STRONGER every day!

Shannon King
530-336-5414 (Office)
844-336-5414 (Toll-Free)
shannon@matteroftheheartcoach.com
matteroftheheartcoach.com

# EPILOGUE

*"The harder the conflict, the more glorious the triumph."*

~ Thomas Paine (1737 - 1809)

English-Activist.

**"YOU DIDN'T THINK** God was going to let us write a book about moving through FRAZZLED to FABULOUS without giving us some FRAZZLED, did you?"

Shannon asked this question during one of our Monday morning collaboration calls. Our Monday or Friday morning calls were used to catch up, encourage, and hold each other accountable in our endeavors. In our sharing this particular Monday, we began to realize we were all experiencing FRAZZLED on various levels.

The world had been thrust into the COVID pandemic about nine months earlier. Everyone was trying to figure out how to deal with all the changes, fears, and unknowns that came with it. Like everyone else, we were doing the same.

With an 'aha,' we recognized the opportunity for FRAZZLED is never-ending, and FABULOUS isn't a destination. We weren't writing about arriving…we were writing about the journey.

We are now only a few months away from the beginning of the third year of the world still struggling with the ongoing COVID concerns. This anthology has been birthed during this uncertain time in our history and the message seems even more important than when it was first conceived.

Like you, the current shadow of uncertainty mingles with the busyness, interruptions, and sometimes tragedies of daily life. During the creation of this anthology, we have experienced health challenges, physical pain, relationship revamping, families relocating, and loss of loved ones.

And, in all of this, there is also light. Whether you call that light God, Love, Spirit, or what resonates within your soul, there is always light. There are all the little things that are often overshadowed, which show us how much we are loved. We have also been blessed with weddings, the building of businesses, revamping of relationships, and good health. Most importantly, we acknowledged our blessings of love, connections, and community.

It is the challenges where we choose to be vulnerable, extract the knowledge, and rise up stronger. It is the blessings that we choose to recognize, be grateful for, knowing they help move us through frazzled to fabulous.

Our encouragement to you is to choose this journey for yourself. Live your life always moving towards fabulous. From our hearts to yours, we love you!

# SPONSOR SPOTLIGHTS

## EUROPA VILLAGE WINERY & RESORT

We had a vision of bringing together the high standards and values of traditional European wine making with the beauty and richness of one of the most ideal wine growing regions in American—the Temecula Valley wine Country in Southern California. The newest addition to Europa Village, Bolero is a place for the young at heart. This lively Spanish winery is a full-bodied experience vibrant with rich colors, bold flavors, and an air of spontaneity.

Indulge in tapas and microbrews at Bolero Restaurante, delight in the luscious flavors of Bolero wines throughout the village, and savor the experience at Brio, a Spanish boutique offering olive oil tastings and mementos from your travels. Step into old-world Spain as you revel in a backdrop of cypress and olive trees, fountains, and wrought iron, and breathe in the rich smells of leather and wood. Whether you're simply escaping to our borders for the day or continuing your journey at one of our private casitas or event spaces, adventure awaits at Bolero…set to the tune of a flamenco guitar.

Yesika Lavyn
Director of Catering & Sales
951.506.1818 ext. 104
yesika@europavillage.com | EuropaVillage.com
41150 Via Europa
Temecula, CA 92591

# WOMEN ORGANIZING WOMEN

**Mission:** Women Organizing Women mission focuses on three core areas:

1) Evangelistic outreach- Sharing the good news about Jesus Christ for community service events, seminars, workshops, youth camps and more.
2) mentorship and coaching- mentorship for young ladies ages 13 to 25 through various programs and activities. Coaching assistance for women leaders such as business development and strategies, platforms to build relationships, networking, call promotion and inspiration affirmations.
3) Support- provide globalize aid to women and children through food sourcing, housing, training and other resources

Women Organizing Women Inc.

41765 Rider Way,

Temecula California. 92590

## CASTLE & COOKE MORTGAGE – MURRIETA

Castle & Cooke
MORTGAGE

**Mission:** Providing the opportunity for homeownership for all who desire. Bringing a serving heart to the table to make dreams come true. Creating sustainable financial foundations through the benefits of homeownership.

Castle & Cooke Mortgage - Murrieta
Branch NMLS ID #2090708
Cea-Jae Howie- Branch Manager - NMLS # 258108

## EMBRACING YOUR ESSENCE

Patsy Sanders

EMBRACING YOUR ESSENCE IS BEAUTIFUL

Embracing Your Essence has you being seen as your most authentic, beautiful self. What you wear matters. Everyone deserves to be confident, approachable, and attractive.

Fashion is a look, not an age, size, name brand or price tag.

Through my six-week *Inspire Your Style Academy* people discover their element and learn how to shop…where they become the masterpiece—and their inspiring style, aligned with their element— becomes the frame that has them be seen, heard, and valued.

Patsy Sanders

International Image Style Expert, Master Hair Stylist,
Inspirational Speaker

Embracing Your Essence

https://embracingyouressence.com

patsy@embracingyouressence.com

707-889-9600

Thank you so much for reading *The Journey is Yours to Take,* and I trust you find merit in the fact that you too can CHOOSE TO MOVE THROUGH FRAZZLED TO FABULOUS. As writers, we rely on those who have read our anthology to be the voice that validates the work we've done. I would be so honored if you would write an honest review on the retail site where you purchased your copy.

I also hope you were inspired by my chapter, "Where I am Meant to Be—Even if Perhaps Only for a Moment." Where I talk about how I embrace change, have come to recognize my life of whimsy…my path to enduring, embracing, and engaging in change. I wonder, were you inspired to consider the changes imposed upon you the past few years or to imagine the transitions you crave as a result? Are you (craving/striving/longing/seeking or interested) to shift your circumstances? Do you now wish to explore the amazing benefits from nature surrounding you, ways to contribute to yourself and others, and how joy and whimsy can accompany your everyday? I would love to offer that, and more!

First, I would love to stay connected with you as a reader of our anthology and know the chapters held some great gems that will have shifted you from FRAZZLED, and on a journey to a FABULOUS life you so richly deserve.

I would also like to invite you to take advantage of an offer provided only to those who have finished reading it. If you would like to further explore how to design your Goalden Life, through goal setting, letting go, and celebrating yourself with simple, personal, and effective formulas, contact me at:

annmarie@mattersofgray.com for a complimentary session. Put The Journey is Yours to Take in the subject line, so I don't miss your request!